First published in 2005 by New Holland Publishers (UK) Ltd
London • Cape Town • Sydney • Auckland
Garfield House, 86–88 Edgware Road, London W2 2EA, United Kingdom
www.newhollandpublishers.com
80 McKenzie Street, Cape Town 8001, South Africa
Level 1, Unit 4, 14 Aquatic Drive, Frenchs Forest, NSW 2086, Australia
218 Lake Road, Northcote, Auckland
Copyright © 2005 text AG&G Books
The right of David Squire to be identified as author of this work has been asserted by him in
accordance with the Copyright, Designs and Patents Act 1988.
Copyright © 2005 illustrations and photographs New Holland Publishers (UK) Ltd
Copyright © 2005 New Holland Publishers (UK) Ltd

ISBN 1 8   8
10 9 8 7 6   2 1

Editorial D   n: Rosemary Wilkinson Senior Editor: Clare Hubbard Production: Hazel Kirkman
Desi   gewater Illustrations: Dawn Brend, Gill Bridgewater, Coral Mula and Ann Winterbotham
            pland Photographs: see page 80
            y Pica Digital Pte Ltd, Singapore
            nd in Malaysia by Times Offset (M) Sdn. Bhd.

      in this book is true and complete to the best of our knowledge. All recommendations
    ut guarantee on the part of the authors and the publishers. The authors and publishers
    ility for damages or injury resulting from the use of this information.

The
SMALL GARDEN

**The essential guide to designing,
creating, planting, improving and
maintaining small gardens**

David Squire

Series editors: A. & G. Bridgewater

NEW HOLLAND

ontents

Author's foreword

Whatever a garden's size, many home gardeners repeatedly yearn for a larger area where, perhaps, a wider range of plants can be grown. Yet it can be just as satisfying to accept a small garden and to cultivate it intensively and in an inspirational way.

By their nature, small gardens sometimes have the bonus of creating unforeseen gardening possibilities; whereas in a large area gardening is mainly at ground level, in small spaces vertical as well as overhead gardening become considerations. Wall shrubs are ideal for clothing walls, while climbers are superb for walls, arches and romantic arbours.

Attractive paths help to unify even the smallest garden, and if the area is exceptionally small a patio or courtyard for growing plants in containers can be an answer

to creating colour throughout the year. Indeed, container gardening with hanging-baskets, windowboxes, wall-baskets, tubs and pots is an inspirational yet practical and popular way to garden.

Many shrubs and small trees have small-garden qualities, including being diminutive or growing only slowly. Additionally, they need varied seasonal interests, whether from flowers, leaves, berries or their bark. Being easy to establish and not having an invasive nature are two other useful qualities. Plants with these attributes are described and recommended in this all-colour, detailed and abundantly illustrated book.

With this book by your side, no small garden need be left bare and neglected. There are exciting and colourful possibilities within every garden, whatever its size or shape.

Plant names

Currently recommended botanical names for plants are given throughout this book. Additionally, where earlier and perhaps better known botanical names are still used, these too are included so that you will instantly know the plants being discussed.

Measurements

Both metric and imperial measurements are given throughout this book – for example, 1.8 m (6 ft).

SEASONS

Throughout this book, advice is given about seasonal tasks. Because of global and even regional variations in climate and temperature, the four main seasons have been used, with each subdivided into 'early', 'mid-' and 'late' – for example, early spring, mid-spring and late spring. These 12 divisions of the year can be applied to the appropriate calendar months in your local area, if you find this helps.

Small but refined

Small gardens, when compared with a similarly sized area within a large garden, encourage and need greater gardening involvement, especially when creating a well-admired display throughout the year. Parts of a large garden often escape rigorous and detailed assessment from visitors and there is always the explanation of it being too large. Within a small garden, you must be prepared for continuous and detailed involvement.

Will it need less attention?

OPPORTUNITIES AND CONSTRAINTS

Constructing a lightly shaded patio, perhaps alongside raised beds and with a small pond generating summer interest, is idyllic – and just one opportunity in a small garden. Additionally, there are plants in containers, many colourful and fragrant and acting as reminders of warmer climates. Therefore, be prepared to spend more money than for an equivalent area in a larger garden. Small is beautiful, but sometimes more expensive.

WHAT'S POSSIBLE?

Clearly, garden features that demand unrestricted space are not possible in a small or even moderately sized garden, but many others can be considered. Some of these have a novel nature that would be too expensive to attempt on a large scale, but in a restricted area are just right. These include Japanese and Mediterranean gardens, as well as draughtboard (checkerboard) and cartwheel herb gardens. There are many other features to consider – see pages 4–5.

↗ *Beds and borders alongside houses can be drenched in colour throughout summer. Use a range of plants, from summer-flowering bedding plants to herbaceous perennials.*
← *Spring-flowering bulbs, such as bright-faced Daffodils in a variety of containers, are also welcome.*

LAWN OR PATIO?

In many gardens, both a lawn and a patio are practical features. A lawn unites a garden and creates an attractive foil for borders and beds, whereas a patio is much needed as a year-round, all-weather surface, as well as for summer relaxation. Therefore, in a small garden it is a lawn that is least necessary. This also saves on the storage of lawn tools and mowers – and, perhaps, fuel.

CREATING SPACE

Even in a small garden it is possible to create an impression of space. Aim to have an open area in the centre of the garden, surrounded by plants or features that do not obstruct views to the full extent of the garden. Ponds encourage a perception of space, with the benefit of reflected light creating an impression of an even larger area.

CREATING SURPRISE

There is a delicate balance in a small garden between creating space and ensuring surprise. Both are essential and the surprise element is best near to the edges of the garden, where perhaps a small leaf-clad arch or screen can be combined with perimeter fencing or a wall. A free-standing trellis, dressed with leafy or flowering climbers, is another way to create surprise.

CREATING PRIVACY

Quiet areas are essential in gardens and privacy has healing and supportive properties. Contemplative areas encourage relaxation; leafy vertical and overhead screens ensure seclusion, especially in summer and when clothed with leaves. *Humulus lupulus* 'Aureus' (Yellow-leaved Hop) is ideal for summer privacy; for all-year screening large-leaved variegated Ivies are better.

Need a shed?

in a large garden, a shed is essential as a place for keeping tools, pots and composts, as well as other equipment. In a small garden, consider a combined summerhouse and shed, or even just rely on a garage, if you have one. See page 76.

Types of small garden

Does small mean restricted opportunities?

Opportunities for creating an exciting but small garden are wide, and apart from vast vistas there are styles and designs to suit most tastes, but on a reduced scale. On these pages there is a pictorial display of a range of diminutive gardens, with descriptions and ideas for many others. Few small gardens are totally devoted to one of these styles, but nevertheless they provide an insight into ways to make a small garden beautiful, functional and exciting.

SMALL-GARDEN STYLES

Informal

↘ These have a casual feel that encourages a relaxed and informal ambience. There is nothing symmetrical about them. Instead, beds are irregularly shaped, with curved patios and informal paths. Shrubs and trees have relaxed habits, with other plants creating further informality. Avoid the creation of straight lines.

Formal

↘ Gardens with a formal nature have straight or clinically curved lines, produced by plants as well as paths and patio edges. Regimentation is often produced by seasonal plants, such as bulbs and biennials in spring displays and half-hardy bedding plants throughout summer. Such gardening enables colour schemes to be changed from one year to another (see pages 34–35).

Mediterranean

↘ With the onset of warmer summers, many gardeners nostalgically like to recall the endless blue skies, warm breezes and little rain of Mediterranean holidays. Choose a combination of plants in pots, window-boxes and hanging-baskets, with shrubs that have silver-coloured or aromatic leaves. Silver leaves reflect hot sunshine, while aromatic leaves create a barrier of oils above their surfaces (see page 24).

Japanese

Japanese gardens exude peace, serenity and contemplation. They have a simple yet planned nature, with involvement from gravel, water, small trees, bamboos and plants in containers. Diminutive fountains and ponds are sometimes possible in small gardens, but if this is difficult the illusion of flowing water can be created by coloured shale (see page 25).

English-style flower borders

↘ This type of flower border has a relaxed, informal and floriferous nature throughout summer. The borders are packed mostly with herbaceous plants that die down in autumn and send up fresh shoots in spring (see pages 18–19).

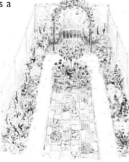

WATER GARDENING

The shape and extent of a garden pond can be matched to a garden's size as well as its style. If space is a problem, consider a miniature pond in a tub or a pebble feature with water gently splashing onto pebbles. This design is ideal for homes with young, inquisitive children who could easily fall into a large pond.

You can use fountains – as well as water spouting out of a wall-secured feature such as a lion's head – to create height. However, try to ensure that water does not splash onto any Waterlily flowers.

FRONT GARDENS

Even the narrowest and smallest front garden can be made attractive. If a small, grassed area is not possible, paving with cobbles in an attractive pattern creates a base for plants in containers (see pages 26–27 for ideas).

If flower beds are possible, create height by planting a standard rose; even better, if space allows, use a weeping rose that will harmonize with ornate, older-style properties.

Where standing areas for cars have meant the demolition of front gardens, consider gravel or paving slabs. Flexible pavers on a thick base can also be used.

Plants in containers revitalize front gardens

CONTAINER GARDENING

Windowboxes drench windows in radiant colour

Hanging-baskets create colour at eye height

Strawberries in pots always attract attention

Few facets of gardening are as popular and versatile as growing plants in containers and positioning them in an attractive way on patios and in other places around a house. Some displays are seasonal, while shrubs, trees and bamboos in tubs become permanent features (see pages 26–27).

BALCONIES AND ROOF GARDENS

Balconies are more popular than roof gardens, which for practical purposes demand strong, waterproof flooring (permission may be needed for its use). Many flats, however, have balconies that are ideal for plants in containers. Ensure that plants cannot fall from the balcony, or be dislodged by violent storms. Positioning troughs on the balcony's base and allowing stems to trail through the balustrade creates colour which can be admired from below.

Balconies are easily clothed in colour

Roof gardens are superb during summer

LOW-MAINTENANCE GARDENS

Whatever a garden's size, short-cut and time-saving gardening is essential for families with busy lifestyles. A garden's design and the use of mechanical equipment can ease time pressures. For example, installing lawn edgings that suit equipment used to trim long grass saves many hours of work throughout a year. Within this book there are ideas about easy gardening maintenance.

SECLUDED AND PRIVATE GARDENS

Increasingly, gardens are outdoor living areas, and to enable them to function in this way seclusion and privacy are essential. Privacy up to head height is easily created by screens, fences and walls, but where neighbours are able to peer from overhead, the creation of seclusion is more difficult. Proprietary awnings attached to a house are useful, while leafy pergolas are another solution. Constructing an arbour a little way into a garden is another possibility.

FOOD-PRODUCING GARDENS

Growing vegetables and fruits in containers never fails to attract attention in small gardens. Apple trees are possible in tubs and large pots, strawberries in barrels and hanging-baskets, and potatoes, lettuces and tomatoes in growing-bags. In small areas – perhaps against fences and walls – cordon, espalier and fan-trained fruit trees are space-savers.

WILDLIFE GARDENS

Wildlife gardens do not have to be large to attract butterflies and other insects, as well as birds and small mammals.

Healing gardens

Plants have a significant influence on our lives, and not just through their well-publicized medicinal qualities. The colours of flowers influence lives. For example, massed red is claimed to raise blood pressure and increase pulse rates, while blue has a soothing effect. Fragrance, sound, shape and texture also influence our lives.

Range of plants for small gardens

What types of plants are best?

Many plants are suitable for small gardens. They range from bulbs and diminutive rock garden plants to herbaceous perennials, summer-flowering bedding plants and miniature and slow-growing dwarf conifers. Additionally, there are superbly attractive small shrubs and trees for space-restricted areas, but they need to be selected with greater care than those plants that are naturally short-lived and can be easily replaced within a few years.

An eye-catching combination of handsome foliage and flowers.

How long do plants live?

Some plants are ephemeral and are replaced during the following year, while others are woody and live for many years.

Annuals: *short-lived* – raised from seeds; they produce flowers and die during the same year.

Biennials: *two seasons* – raised from seeds one year and flower and die during the following year.

Herbaceous perennials: *3–4 years before division is needed* – plants die down to ground level each autumn and reappear during the following spring.

Shrubs: *10 or more years* – woody, perennial plants with stems growing from soil level and without a trunk.

Trees: *20 or more years* – woody, with a single stem (trunk) joining the branches to the roots.

Climbers: annual (see above), herbaceous (see above) or woody and perennial, and living for ***10 or more years***.

Conifers: *15 or more years* – either tree or shrub-like, with an evergreen or deciduous nature.

Bamboos: *15 or more years* – thicket-forming, with stiff, upright, hollow stems.

Rock garden plants: *3 or more years* – range of types, from alpines to small border perennials.

Bulbs: *short-lived* – but produce further bulbs around them that develop into flowering-size bulbs.

Plants to seek

With such a wide range of plants available, it can be difficult to make a successful selection. Here are a few tips for a small garden.

- **Rapid establishment** is essential to ensure that the garden is soon cloaked in colourful and attractively shaped plants. Quick establishment depends on thorough pre-planting soil preparation and buying healthy plants (see page 15 for what to look for when buying).

- **Slow-growing plants** ensure that their neighbours – as well as the garden in general – are not rapidly swamped with branches and stems.

- **Non-invasive plants** are essential in small gardens to ensure that they will neither block drains nor quickly spread into neighbouring gardens.

- **Plants with two or more display qualities** are desirable when creating attractive gardens in small areas.

- **Plants that produce limited debris** each year are essential in town gardens, where the disposal of garden waste can be a problem.

- **Plants that do not encourage the presence of pests and diseases** are desirable. Some plants attract pests and diseases and these should be avoided.

CONIFER CONFLICT!

Do not plant the fast-growing, hedging conifer Cupressocyparis leylandii *(Leyland Cypress) in your garden. Within ten years it will need to be removed.*

AVOIDING BAMBOO BLUNDERS

Bamboos are superb garden plants, creating interest throughout the year with their colourful leaves and canes. Some have invasive roots, however; here are ways around the problem.

Select problem-free bamboos (see page 50).

Plant suitable bamboos in containers (see page 50).

Install bamboo barriers (see page 50).

PICTORIAL SURVEY OF PLANTS

Small gardens can be just as colourful and exciting as large ones. Indeed, when a colour-packed small garden is compared with the same area in a large garden it is often more attractive. Success is a matter of *concentrated gardening endeavour* and *selecting the right plants*. This fully illustrated book will help you create such an exciting garden.

Shrubs

There are small evergreen and deciduous shrubs for planting in small gardens. Some shrubs, such as *Fuchsia magellanica*, are not frost hardy; others, like the evergreen *Aucuba japonica* 'Variegata' (Spotted Laurel), create colour throughout the year. The diminutive *Hypericum olympicum* is low-growing, with yellow flowers in mid- and late summer.

Small trees

Many trees are low growing and those with a dome-shaped outline and weeping habit, such as *Betula pendula* 'Youngii' (Young's Weeping Birch), are especially attractive. This Birch helps to unify a garden and is also suitable for planting as a specimen tree on a lawn.

Climbers

Large-flowered Clematis are ideal for clambering over a trellis in a small garden. There are many varieties and colours from which to choose.

Wall shrubs

Evergreen Ceanothus is superb for creating colour against a wall in late spring and early summer. Select a sheltered wall in full sun.

Plants for containers

Long-term plants for growing in containers include the deciduous, low, rounded and dome-shaped *Acer palmatum* 'Dissectum Atropurpureum', with its finely dissected, bronze-red leaves.

Rock-garden plants

Small rock-garden plants are ideal for gardens with little space, and a wide range of different types can be planted in a small area. Also add small bulbs and miniature and slow-growing conifers.

Miniature and slow-growing conifers

These varied evergreens have a dwarf or slow-growing habit. They can be planted in rock gardens, mixed with heathers or planted on their own alongside paths.

Herbaceous perennials

Many of these reliable garden plants are suitable for small gardens, including *Hemerocallis* (Day Lilies) and the superb *Alchemilla mollis* (Lady's Mantle), which is ideal for planting alongside path and border edges. Hostas are other reliable border plants and can also be planted in containers on patios.

Spring-flowering plants

A combination of Tulips and Wallflowers never fails to create colour in beds and borders in spring. These plants are inexpensive to buy and easy to change each year.

Summer-flowering bedding plants

These are raised each year from seeds and include plants as varied and colourful as Petunias, Lobelias and Marigolds.

Vegetables, fruit and herbs

The range of food plants for small gardens is wide, from strawberries in planters to salad crops in sheltered beds. Dwarfing rootstocks enable apples and other tree fruits to be cultivated.

Water plants

Marginal and water plants are available for planting near and in ponds. By choosing suitable varieties, Waterlilies can be grown in many different depths of water.

Bamboos

Several bamboos are small and as well as being planted in garden soil can be put into ornamental containers. Many of them bear colourful leaves and canes.

Choice of infrastructure

Are special designs possible?

When planning the infrastructure of a small garden, there is usually more money available for the construction of each square metre or yard than for a large garden, where economies generally have to be made. Additionally, because the area is small, immediate and more distinctive visual impact is needed. Garden centres and builder's yards, as well as catalogues from magazines and newspapers, will give you an idea of the materials available.

FENCING CHECKS

You may have inherited an attractive small garden and initially decided not to make radical changes, but if you have children and dogs it is worth checking fences.

- Fencing posts broken at ground level can be repaired by cutting off the base and fitting a spike-ended, metal, post-base. Alternatively, bolt a concrete or wooden post to sound wood and re-concrete into the ground.
- Arris rails broken at their joints with vertical posts can be repaired by screwing a metal bracket to the post.
- Arris rails which have snapped along their lengths also can be repaired by metal brackets.

Walls smothered in flowering climbers, such as Roses, Clematis and Honeysuckle, create colour as well as informality.

Structural elements to consider

- **Decking:** raised or at ground level – page 69.
- **Edgings:** wide range, including concrete and wood – page 75.
- **Paths:** surfaces and durability – pages 62–63.
- **Patios, courtyards and terraces:** wide choice – page 64.
- **Pergolas, trellises and arches:** for small gardens – pages 72–73.
- **Porches and entrances:** decorative features – page 74.
- **Sheds and greenhouses:** practical features – pages 76–77.
- **Steps:** practical yet attractive – page 68.
- **Walls and fences:** garden perimeters – pages 66–67.

PROBLEMS WITH CLAY

Increasingly, high temperatures combined with limited summer rain causes clay to shrink radically. Where foundations of buildings are deep, this creates few problems but, when paving slabs on a patio or path have only a thin concrete base, eventually they deform and rock. First-aid treatment is to lift and re-cement individual slabs. For a longer-term solution, you will need to lift all the slabs and provide a thicker base for the complete patio or path.

DISPOSING OF RUBBISH

Getting rid of garden rubbish can be a problem, but there are several solutions.

- **Hire a skip** – check that it is insured to be left on a public road and whether lights are needed. Mini- and large skips are usually available.
- **Builder's bags** – these are increasingly used to deliver building materials, as well as collecting rubbish. They are about a metre/yard square and deep. Check with your local builder's merchant.
- **Local authority** – may provide a rubbish-collection service.

INFRASTRUCTURE EXAMPLES

A small garden

↘ Within informal gardens, a surprisingly wide range of features can be included in a casual yet purposeful manner. The pergola acts as a focal point.

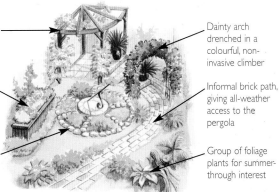

A corner pergola is an unusual feature that demands attention

Large troughs or raised beds enable plants to be easily seen

Culinary herb garden formed of large pebbles in a cartwheel shape

Dainty arch drenched in a colourful, non-invasive climber

Informal brick path, giving all-weather access to the pergola

Group of foliage plants for summer-through interest

A small front garden

↘ Most small front gardens have a formal character, with plants in rows and neat roadside edgings. Porches help to create focal points for paths.

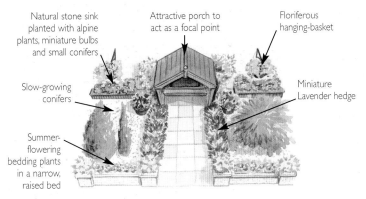

Natural stone sink planted with alpine plants, miniature bulbs and small conifers

Slow-growing conifers

Summer-flowering bedding plants in a narrow, raised bed

Attractive porch to act as a focal point

Floriferous hanging-basket

Miniature Lavender hedge

A small courtyard

↘ Courtyards are summer-leisure areas as well as places where plants can be grown. By their nature, courtyards are private areas, with complete seclusion.

Gap in courtyard floor for a small, woody climber or shrub to be grown

Collection of wall pots and baskets, packed with summer flowers

Pebbled area, contrasting with square paving slabs

Corner wall-baskets and other wire-framed plant supports

Bricks in herring-bone pattern, contrasting with paving and pebbles

Miniature water feature, with water gushing into a brick-made, waterproof base

THINK ABOUT THE PLANTS

Don't separate the selection of plants from getting the infrastructure right.
- If you like relaxed plants such as bamboos, ferns and ornamental grasses, you will want an informal garden to complement them.
- For clinical and regimented displays of summer-flowering bedding plants, you will need a formal garden.

INFRASTRUCTURE FOR ROOF GARDENS

Persistent and buffeting wind combined with strong sunlight make roof gardens difficult but exciting places for gardening. Additionally, consider the following constructional questions.

- Permission may be required from the building's owner, as well as from local authorities. Also, check the thoughts of neighbours – it may not impress them.

- The weight of the flooring needs to be light but strong – check with a structural engineer if in doubt.

- The weight of pots and other containers – when full of soil-based compost and after being watered – may be excessive.

- Don't damage felt roofs.

- Make sure excess water is adequately drained.

- A sturdy screen is usually needed to filter strong wind. Make sure it cannot be blown away and cause damage to people and property.

MAKING THE MOST OF BALCONIES

These are more sheltered than a roof garden, and with a base that is firm and secure. However, a sun-facing position will rapidly dry compost.
- If the balcony does not have a roof, fit a collapsible sunshade.
- Where a balcony has a roof, but strong, late-evening sunlight still causes dazzle, you can fit a frill to the balcony's upper edge.
- Always make sure that water cannot drip on people or balconies below. Wherever possible, stand pots in large, plastic saucers.

Problems and opportunities

Can all sites be made attractive?

With all sites there are problems and opportunities, and sometimes areas that initially appear totally inhospitable eventually produce the most interesting and distinctive gardens – unique and full of character. Creating height through arches, trellises and pergolas draws attention away from exceptionally narrow or short gardens, while a levelled area on a steep slope becomes idyllic when turned into a leisure feature, especially if illuminated at night.

Use climbers to cloak eyesores and barren walls. Hanging-baskets and windowboxes can be used in a similar way.

Annuals are sown in spring each year to create an inexpensive yet vibrantly coloured feast of flowers.

Raised decking is ideal for creating a distinctive feature, perhaps alongside a stream or a colourful garden pond.

TOO SMALL?

Logically, there is a size when it is near impossible to create an area in which plants can be grown. Yet many successful gardens are created in areas at the entrances to basement flats, where both space and light are limited. In small areas ideals are limited, but a few decorative pots, a hanging-basket and windowbox can be just as cherished as an extensive and well-manicured lawn is to a croquet devotee.

SEEING THE OPPORTUNITIES

The ability to recognize hidden opportunities in potential gardens is, in part, gained by looking at other gardens, both locally and nationally. Some large display gardens even have areas where a range of small gardens are featured; even if one of them in its entirety does not suit you, an amalgam of several elements may be practical in your garden. Have a sketch-pad or camera handy and take a few notes that later give clues to opportunities.

WASHING-LINE PROBLEMS

Years ago, when moving to a new house and being presented with a barren garden the first demand was for a washing-line. Unfortunately, this usually determined the position of the main path and dictated the nature of the garden. Fortunately, washing-line spinners have eliminated this problem. Even if initially put in the wrong place, they can be easily moved and reconcreted into position.

SHADY OR SUNNY?

A garden's aspect is not usually the first consideration when moving to a new house. Whether it is fully exposed to sunlight or shaded by trees or neighbouring buildings can be a lottery that brings both problems and opportunities. There are plants that delight in full sun, while others prefer to grow in shade. The light or shade preferences of many plants are detailed in the plant directory (see pages 34–59).

The degree and nature of light and shade in a garden varies from one part of a day to another.

- **Full sun:** many plants thrive in full sun, especially if regularly watered. Those native to hot countries and with hot-climate adaptations such as silvery, hairy or aromatic leaves are first choices, but even these need help when getting established. Regular watering and yearly mulching are two moisture-saving tasks.

- **Light shade:** most plants thrive in a combination of dappled light and full sun. Unless there is a large, overhead canopy of leaves from a tree (which also deprives other plants of moisture and nutrients) the brightest time is during the middle part of a day.

- **Heavy shade:** most decorative garden plants do not grow well or exhibit attractive qualities when in deep shade. Unless the shade comes from a building, thin out an overhead canopy created by trees.

AWKWARDLY SHAPED SITES

Long and narrow

⬎ Create the impression of a shorter garden by dividing it into several units, each with a unique feel. In a small garden, a free-standing trellis, perhaps combined with a leaf-drenched arch, takes up less space than a dense hedge. Create mystery by varying the position of a linking path, making it impossible to see the bottom of the garden from the house.

Short and wide

⬎ Accentuate the shortness by erecting a head-high screen of leafy or flowering climbers across the garden, so that the boundary cannot be seen. Ensure that the screen is not too high, because a glimpse of openness beyond the garden removes any feeling of claustrophobia. A well-kept lawn creates an impression of space, while a bench positioned close to the screen forms a focal point.

Steep slopes

⬎ Slopes provide added interest in a garden, although moving from one level to another can sometimes be difficult – especially as age progresses. Flights of 6–8 steps – with a resting landing between them – make slopes easier to negotiate.

Creating a flattened leisure area on a steep slope helps to split it up. Where possible, position this feature level with head height when viewed from a patio around the house.

Terracing slopes

Brick retaining walls have a formal nature and are suited to relatively open areas, whereas old railway sleepers are better for relaxed and informal settings with beds of heathers and deciduous azaleas. Peat-blocks are another solution to soil retention, but not on steep slopes. In open areas, slopes can be grassed, with level areas interspersed with 45° slopes. Hover mowers are ideal for cutting grass on slopes.

SOIL PROBLEMS

Soils vary in their nature; most are neutral and neither acid nor alkaline. Others are well drained, some waterlogged. Occasionally they are hot and dry. Plants that prefer specific soils are indicated in the plant directory (see pages 34–59).

- **Acid soils:** these are soils with a pH below about 6.5. Acidity can be corrected by dusting the surface with hydrated lime or ground limestone in winter, after digging. However, some plants – such as Rhododendrons and Azaleas – demand acid soils.
- **Alkaline (chalky) soils:** these have a pH above 7.0. Chalky soils can be corrected by used acidic fertilizers such as sulphate of ammonia, plus applications of peat. Many plants grow well in chalky soils.
- **Neutral soils:** these are soils with a pH of 7.0, although most plants grow well in a pH between 6.5 and 7.0.

Exposed and windswept sites

Newly planted as well as established plants are often damaged by cold, searing winds. Hedges filter the wind and can be used to make gardens more congenial for tender plants. Walls create barriers and encourage swirling eddies on the lee side, as well as buffeting on the windward face.

Coastal gardens

Salt-laden wind is present along coastal strips as well as a few kilometres or miles inland. Some plants tolerate these conditions, while others have their leaves damaged. Coastal plants for forming attractive hedges in warm areas include *Fuchsia magellanica* (Hardy Fuchsia) and *Tamarix ramosissima* (Tamarisk; also known as *Tamarix pentandra*).

Design and planning

Is detailed planning essential?

For many people, gardens just evolve or are a continuation of one that was inherited during a change of house ownership. When starting from scratch, however, a plan is essential for the major infrastructure including, if desired, the size, shape and position of a lawn. Pencilling in positions and sizes of shrubs and trees also helps to generate thoughts of specific plants. See the plant directory (pages 34–59) for guidance on choosing plants for small gardens.

ASSESSING SLOPES

Differences in levels are difficult to judge without specialized equipment. Home gardeners, however, can use a hosepipe to assess a slope. Tie one end to a post inserted at the highest position. Trail the other end to the lower position and raise it (attached to a post) to about the same height. Fill the pipe with water until both ends are full; a piece of clear plastic tubing in each end makes this easier to judge. The height of water in the lower pipe (minus the hosepipe's height at the top end) indicates the difference in levels.

MAPPING OUT THE AREA

Create a detailed and precise plan on graph paper

If the area has a regular shape, transfer the garden's size and shape directly to graph paper. For irregular outlines, use a hosepipe. Lay it straight down the middle and every 2–3 metres or yards insert a cane. By measuring laterally from the hosepipe, irregularly shaped perimeters can be recorded and marked on graph paper.

MARKING IN YOUR DESIGN

When the shape and size of the garden have been marked on graph paper, it is possible to transfer your desired features (see above right) onto the plan. First, photocopy the graph paper several times so that different sketches can be made.

Gathering inspirations

All members of a family believe themselves to be supremely gifted when choosing garden features. Family involvement is essential, however, and, if everyone notes their preferences, a sensible list of priorities can be created.

When planning a family garden, remember that within several years a play area for children will not be needed. Therefore, initially shape such an area so that another feature, perhaps a garden pond or scree bed, can be later slotted into its place.

Storm water

As global warming increases, redirecting surface water from heavy rainstorms will be necessary. Essentially, water needs to be directed away from houses and their foundations. Wherever possible, install drains or enable water to seep into soil, rather than running off paved areas and directly up to a house, where it can enter through air ventilation bricks and doors.

STOPCOCKS AND DRAINS

Mark stopcocks and manhole-covers on the plan. A stopcock for a mains water supply is usually positioned just inside your property's boundary and next to a pavement or road. These cannot be moved. Manholes also cannot be moved, but their covers can be raised and merged into a drive or standing area for cars. This is usually a job for a builder.

PLANNING CHECKLIST

DO:

✔ Do choose small and slow-growing shrubs and trees for small gardens. Excessively pruning large shrubs and trees, with a view to keeping them small, does not work.

✔ Do create a garden that is unique to you – a wide range of opportunities are described on pages 4–5.

✔ Do consider space-saving wall-trained fruit trees for small gardens. Fruit can also be grown in large containers on a patio (see pages 56–57).

✔ Do install garden lighting as it extends the period of outdoor-living during summer (see page 14).

DON'T:

✗ Don't plant hedges less than half their expected width next to a boundary.

✗ Don't plant trees with spreading branches close to a boundary. Your neighbour will be entitled to cut them off, spoiling the tree's shape.

✗ Don't plant invasive bamboos near to a boundary (see page 50 for non-invasive types).

✗ Don't drain water so that it runs on to neighbouring gardens.

✗ Don't position patios and terraces directly on boundary lines as it may then be impossible to erect a fence or trellis.

Getting equipped

Well-made garden tools that suit your height and build are an investment for life and a pleasure to use. Always buy the best quality that you can afford; stainless-steel types are expensive and durable, but others – perhaps with an anodized surface – are just as long-lived if they are regularly cleaned after use and stored in a dry, well-ventilated shed. Garden spades and forks are both available in several sizes, and with a choice of handle types.

Are garden tools expensive?

BASIC GARDENING TOOLS

Digging and soil preparation

Trowel

Hand fork

Spade Fork Rake Hoe Wheelbarrow

Garden spades and forks are mainly used to dig soil, while rakes are for levelling. Dutch hoes remove weeds and create a friable surface, and draw hoes form drills, as well as hoeing and removing weeds.

Watering the garden

A stout watering-can is essential for watering trays of young plants before they are planted out – as well as for watering them regularly afterwards. On a large scale, using a hosepipe and sprinkler will make it much easier to care for plants.

Watering-can

Lawn tools

Lawn rake

Edging shears

Edging knife

Spring-, plastic- and rubber-tined lawn rakes are ideal for removing dead grass and leaves, and scattering worm-casts. Edging knives (edging irons) are used to neaten lawn edges, and edging shears are for trimming long grass at the edges.

Pruning and hedging tools

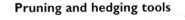

Secateurs Loppers Hedging shears Grecian saw

Electrical hedging shears

Secateurs, both 'bypass' and 'anvil' types, are used for pruning, as are Grecian saws and loppers. Shears are ideal for trimming hedges; electrical ones are best for large hedges.

Greenhouses

In greenhouses, pots and seed-trays are essential, together with dibbers and knives for trimming cuttings. Long-spout watering-cans are useful.

WHEN BUYING GARDEN TOOLS

When buying a garden tool, always check its weight and feel the way it handles. Unless it feels right, leave it alone. Left-handed secateurs are available, and these make pruning much easier for left-handed gardeners.

SAFETY FIRST

Garden tools can be lethal to other people, as well as yourself. When using them, make sure they cannot be tripped over or, in the case of a metal rake, trodden on and quickly knocked upright.

CLEANING AND STORING

Washing and cleaning garden equipment after use extends its life. Dry bright metal surfaces and wipe them with an oily rag. Clean and dry wooden and plastic handles. When not in use, store tools in a dry, well-aerated shed – preferably, hang them up.

Garden spades

Garden spades are the most widely used pieces of garden equipment and their range is wide. Spades are available in several sizes: digging types have blades about 27 x 19 cm (11 x 7½ in), while border models are 23 x 14 cm (9 x 5½ in) and often sold as 'lady's spades'. Some spades have blades with tread-like ledges at the top of the blade, enabling more pressure to be put on the blade while digging, but this makes them more difficult to clean.

Most spades have a 72 cm (28 in) long handle, although others are 82 cm (32 in). There are three different types of handle, and the one to choose is a matter of personal preference. These include T-shaped, D-outlined and D-Y (which is the most popular).

Lighting in a garden

Garden illumination – whether on patios, in borders, among trees or around ornamental ponds as well as submerged – has gained in popularity, and in return for the initial cost and subsequent maintenance makes a garden and patio more attractive and usable over a longer period each day. Additionally, autumn-coloured deciduous trees and frost-covered stems during winter can be highlighted. For barbecue enthusiasts, patio lighting is essential.

Are garden lights worth installing?

ON PATIOS

The edges of patios and terraces can be transformed by low spotlights as well as column types. Also, where a table is present a light that illuminates it is useful for late-evening relaxation. Avoid having cables suspended randomly over a patio.

IN BORDERS

Throughout summer and into autumn, borders of all types – packed solely with herbaceous perennials or a medley of types – benefit from illumination. Flowers and coloured leaves can be given added qualities by lights positioned looking down on plants. Additionally, a few lights within a border create attractive shadows.

Ornamental lights are ideal for patios and terraces.

AROUND PONDS

Whether a garden pond is integrated with a patio or featured in a lawn setting, it will be enhanced by a few strategically placed lights. If a waterfall or cascade feeds water into it, these too can be illuminated. Fountains, with their wide and varying range of spray patterns, are also enhanced.

IN PONDS

Submerged lighting – sometimes coloured in red, green, amber or blue – adds a fresh and often novel quality to ornamental ponds. Some lighting equipment creates a rainbow of changing light. Ensure that the equipment is safely installed.

FLOODLIGHTING TREES AND SHRUBS

Wall- and post-mounted lights create light over a large area, while low-powered coloured lights in a continuous line of up to 40 lamps are possible for stringing between trees. For many gardens, however, a few white spotlights focused upwards and into branches have more appeal.

TYPES OF LIGHTING

The quality and intensity of light is influenced by the source of power – mains, battery or solar.

- **Mains power:** this creates the strongest and most penetrating light and is suitable for large installations and powerful spotlights. It also requires the most careful and thorough installation.
- **Battery power:** the size and quality of the battery determines the power of the light, which slowly diminishes as the battery becomes exhausted. Nevertheless, it is a safe way to have light on a patio or terrace.
- **Solar power:** the penetrative quality of the light is poor, but is useful for highlighting the edges of features, from patios to paths and around ponds. It has the bonus of being powered by the sun and inexpensive to operate.

↙ *Spotlights are ideal for highlighting specific plants, as well as on patios during summer evenings*

↙ *Low-intensity lights on short, supporting stems are good for positioning around either a patio or a garden pond*

↙ *Lantern-type battery lights, with their ornamental appearance, are useful for hanging from trees around a patio*

SAFETY FIRST

Electricity and water are not happy partners and all electrical installations need to be checked over or installed by a competent electrician. Where voltage is reduced through a transformer the risk to yourself and family is less than when the power comes directly from the mains electricity supply.

DO NOT TAKE ANY RISKS – THINK SAFETY FIRST WITH ELECTRICITY AT ALL TIMES.

Choosing and buying plants

Plants can be bought throughout the year and planted whenever the soil and weather allow (see below for times to buy plants). However, for most gardeners spring is the time when thoughts of planting a new border or restructuring a garden are implemented. This timing enables plants to become established before the onset of unfavourable weather in autumn. However, bare-rooted shrubs and trees need to be planted when dormant in winter.

When should I buy plants?

WHERE TO BUY PLANTS

Always buy plants – whether shrubs and trees, herbaceous perennials or bulbs and bedding plants – from reputable sources. You will want to be assured that the plant is correctly labelled as well as healthy.

Garden centres: these mainly sell container-grown plants, and therefore it is essential to visit them in a car, although some offer a local delivery service. Check out the garden centre as well as plants; if it looks neglected and radiates little pride, this may be reflected in the quality of the plants.

Nurseries: these offer bare-rooted as well as container-grown plants. Container-grown types are available throughout the year, and bare-rooted ones in winter only. They can either be collected, or arrangements made for delivery. Some nurseries specialize in specific plants, and this may mean a long journey or buying through a catalogue.

Local shops and markets: a wide range of plants is offered, from container-grown shrubs and herbaceous perennials to biennials and bulbs. Remember, however, to check the plants thoroughly before buying.

Mail order: Many plants, including bare-rooted shrubs, trees and roses, and container-grown shrubs can be bought through mail-order sources. Orders can be given by telephone, fax or post, and paid for by cheque or plastic cards. Most mail-order companies are reputable, but don't forget that you will be buying plants unseen.

WHAT TO LOOK FOR WHEN BUYING SHRUBS AND TREES

Container-grown
↘ *Check that there is no moss on the compost, or masses of roots coming out of the drainage holes in the container.*

Bare-rooted
↘ *Check that the roots are undamaged. Usually, the roots are covered to prevent them becoming dry. Always buy such plants from a reputable source.*

Balled
↘ *Roots are tightly wrapped in hessian. Check that this is not loose and compost has not fallen away. It should be lightly moist.*

Wrapped in polythene
↘ *Stems and shoots are healthy, with moisture-retentive material around roots. Remove packaging as soon as possible.*

TIME OF THE YEAR TO BUY

- Container-grown shrubs, trees, climbers and wall shrubs are sold throughout the year.
- Bare-rooted shrubs, trees and wall shrubs are sold and planted during winter.
- 'Balled' evergreen shrubs and conifers are sold and planted in late summer and early autumn, or in spring.
- Herbaceous plants are mainly sold in early summer.
- Summer-flowering bedding plants are sold in late spring and early summer.
- Rock-garden plants are usually sold in containers in spring or early summer.
- Spring-flowering bulbs are sold in late summer or early autumn, for immediate planting.
- Spring- and early summer-flowering biennials are sold in early autumn, for immediate planting.
- Water-garden plants are usually sold in early summer.

GETTING PLANTS HOME

A car is usually essential. For safe arrival home with plants, do not take children or dogs with you! Make a special visit to buy plants, rather than squeezing them in between other shopping. Cover seats with plastic sheeting.

WHEN PLANTING IS DELAYED

Bare-rooted shrubs and trees can be 'heeled-in' if soil and weather are not suitable for immediate planting.

- Select a sheltered position with moderately moist soil.
- Dig a trench 30–38 cm (12–15 in) deep, with a sloping side away from prevailing wind.
- Remove packaging and position the roots in the trench.
- Spread friable soil over the roots and slightly firm it; lightly water if dry.
- Plants can be left for several weeks, until soil and weather are suitable for planting.

Looking after plants

Do plants need regular attention?

Plants need careful attention throughout their lives. Summer-flowering bedding plants in containers on a patio need regular watering and removal of dead flowers, while lawns require cutting and edges trimmed; also, trees must be checked to ensure stakes are not rubbing their bark. The gardening year is full of plant maintenance that turns a mediocre garden into one in which you can be especially proud. These pages show how to look after a wide range of plants.

Summer-flowering plants in hanging-baskets, windowboxes, troughs and tubs need watering each day, especially when the weather is hot.

DO ALL PLANTS NEED LOOKING AFTER?

Most garden plants are in an artificial environment, often radically different from their native areas. However, the majority of them are adaptive and grow surprisingly well in alien conditions – but they do benefit from extra care and attention, especially when young and becoming established.

Plants are often expected to create colourful displays year after year, while others are encouraged to put all of their endeavours into a feast of colour during a few summer months.

LOW MAINTENANCE?

Trees, shrubs and conifers need less attention than summer-flowering bedding plants in borders or those planted in containers on a patio, such as hanging-baskets, wall-baskets and windowboxes. Unless these are regularly watered, displays soon fail.

Plants in containers

In winter, prevent compost in tubs and large pots becoming too wet by covering with polythene

- Water plants regularly throughout summer.
- Pinch off growing tips of some summer-flowering plants to encourage bushiness.
- Remove dead flowers to encourage others to develop.
- Regularly feed plants in hanging-baskets, windowboxes, wall-baskets and tubs.
- In winter, cover compost in tubs and large pots which are homes to shrubs and trees to prevent it becoming excessively wet.

In winter, cloak tender shrubs in large containers with straw

Looking after hedges

- Keep the bases of young hedges weed-free – they rob plants of moisture and food.
- Refirm soil around young hedges in spring – use the heel of your shoe.
- Water young hedges to encourage rapid establishment.
- Regularly trim formal hedges to create a neat shape.
- Brush off snow as soon as possible; use a bamboo cane or a soft brush. If left, the weight of snow deforms hedges.
- Use secateurs – rather than hedging shears – to shape and remove straggly shoots from large-leaved, informal hedges. Take care not to shred leaves.

Looking after a lawn

- Regularly water lawns – especially newly established ones – throughout summer.
- Cut lawns throughout summer. During dry, hot summers leave the grass longer and cut less frequently.
- Trim lawn edges to keep the lawn neat. Pick up the cut edgings – if left, they may develop roots.
- Rake and scarify lawns. Additionally, in autumn rake off fallen leaves from nearby trees.
- Aerate and topdress lawns during late summer or early autumn.

Use edging shears to trim long grass along lawn edges

Repairing holes in lawns

1 Place a piece of wood, 25–30 cm (10–12 in) square and 12 mm (½ in) thick, over the hole; use an edging iron to cut around it.

2 Lift out the piece of turf and level the soil.

3 Use the same piece of wood to cut a square of turf from an out-of-the-way position.

4 Place the fresh piece of turf in the hole (above, right) and sprinkle friable soil along the joints. Firm and water the area.

Repairing lawn edges

1 Place a 20–23 cm (8–9 in) wide and 30 cm (12 in) long, 12 mm (½ in) thick piece of wood over the damaged area.

2 Use an edging iron to cut around it.

3 Lift out the tuft and turn it so that the damaged area is towards the lawn's middle.

4 Sprinkle friable soil into the damaged area, firm and dust with lawn seed; gently water.

Levelling bumps and depressions in lawns

1 Use an edging iron to cut a straight line across the bump or depression.

2 Then, use the edging iron to cut several lines, 23 cm (9 in) apart, at right angles to the first line.

3 Peel back the turf and either add or remove soil.

4 Replace the turf, firm and dribble friable soil into the cuts. Water.

Cutting off a large branch

1 Cut off the branch 45–60 cm (1½–2 ft) from the trunk.

2 Use a sharp saw to make a cut on the underside of the branch and close to the trunk.

3 Make the next cut from above. A Grecian saw is ideal for cutting close to a branch or in an awkward position.

4 Use a sharp knife to smooth the cut and its edges. Then, coat with a fungicidal tree paint.

Use an old, clean brush to coat smoothed cuts with a fungicidal paint

Looking after a pond

• Keep the water topped up throughout summer. Evaporation soon lowers the water's surface and may damage plants.

• If ponds need to be emptied and cleaned, choose a warm day in early summer – but first remove the fish.

• In autumn, remove leaves that have fallen into the pond. Also, pull out dead leaves from water plants.

Looking after herbaceous plants

• In late autumn or early spring, remove dead stems and supporting, twiggy sticks (if used).

• In spring, lightly fork the soil. Water the soil and add a mulch. Additionally, some plants need support.

• Throughout summer, remove dead flowers. Keep the soil moist, especially during hot weather.

Looking after annual bedding plants

• These are planted in early summer (after all risk of frost has passed); keep the soil moist, especially during hot weather.

• In mid-summer, scatter a general fertilizer around plants (but not touching) and gently water the soil.

• In autumn, pull up all plants and place on a compost heap.

Looking after biennials

• Plant them in early autumn, as soon as available. Sometimes this is combined with planting bulbs between them.

• Thoroughly water the soil to ensure that plants do not shrivel in hot autumn sunshine.

• In early spring, refirm frost-loosened soil around plants.

• Pull up and discard plants when their displays finish.

Looking after shrubs

• In spring, lightly fork soil around established shrubs. Thoroughly water and add a 7.5–10 cm (3–4 in) thick mulch.

• During hot summers, regularly and thoroughly water the soil, especially for shrubs in flower.

• Prune shrubs as required.

Shrubs such as this Buddleja davidii (Butterfly Bush) need yearly pruning

Cut out 'reverted' shoots from variegated evergreen shrubs

Most Roses need yearly pruning to encourage the regular development of shoots and flowers

Flower gardens

Is a flood of colour possible?

Even in small gardens it is possible to create a miniature, English-style flowering garden, with masses of colour provided mainly by herbaceous plants with help from summer-flowering bedding plants. A wide range of herbaceous perennials is illustrated and discussed on pages 38–41. They create superb displays for 3–4 years before needing to be lifted and divided, while summer-flowering bedding plants are planted fresh each year.

INFORMAL MEDLEYS OF FLOWERING PLANTS

Integrate garden ornaments into flower borders.

Informal medleys of herbaceous perennials, summer-flowering bedding plants, shrubs, small trees, biennials and summer-flowering bulbs are especially popular in small gardens where, perhaps, only one border is possible. These 'mixed' borders create colour over a long period and often enable the inclusion of your most diverse and favourite plants. In a small garden, rely mainly on herbaceous perennials, with just a few shrubs that have a dual quality of flowers and colourful leaves. If some of these plants have fragrant flowers, that is a bonus.

Where bulbs are used in mixed borders, choose mainly summer-flowering types, such as lilies. If spring-flowering bulbs are used, this prevents soil cultivation in early summer. Also, when their leaves have died down there is a risk of damaging the hidden bulbs.

'Mixed' borders have a colourful and vibrant nature.

Floral entrances with climbers and containers

English-style entrances become awash with colour and fragrance from scented flowering climbers, with a variety of container-grown plants adding to the riot of colour.

For formal entrances: large-flowered Clematis: wide range, with a deciduous nature and mainly single flowers, in many colours and often throughout summer.

For semi-formal entrances: *Clematis macropetala*: bushy and deciduous, with light and dark blue, bell-shaped and nodding flowers during late spring and early summer.

For rustic settings: *Lonicera periclymenum* (Woodbine/ Honeysuckle): popular cottage-garden climber – the cultivar 'Belgica' (Early Dutch Honeysuckle) flowers during late spring and early summer, and 'Serotina' (Late Dutch Honeysuckle) from mid-summer to autumn.

Raised beds enable a variety of plants to be seen easily, as well as making gardening more comfortable for people who are confined to wheelchairs or who cannot easily bend down.

HOW TO CREATE A MINIATURE FLOWER GARDEN

Whatever a garden's size, the desire to create masses of colour is paramount, as well as replicating a traditional English-style flower garden with its homely and reassuring nature. In earlier years and on a grand scale, borders were sometimes colour-themed – perhaps mainly white, gold-and-yellow, green or blue – now this is seldom attempted.

Traditionally, herbaceous perennials were grown in double borders, facing each other, separated by a broad grass path and backed by hedges that created shelter and harmonized with colour-themed borders. Nowadays, and on a small scale, this can be replicated by creating borders with small-garden herbaceous perennials (see pages 38–41), a central path and two small lawns on either side of it. Path edgings of summer-flowering bedding plants can be used to introduce further colour.

Adding a paved or bricked surface at the far end of these borders and lawns creates a focal point, as well as a leisure area for an attractive bench.

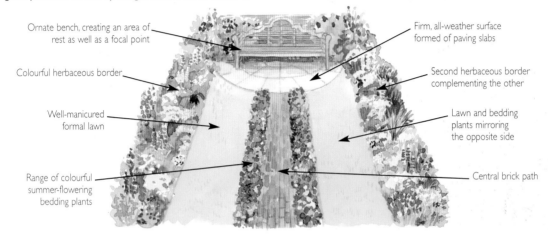

Ornate bench, creating an area of rest as well as a focal point

Colourful herbaceous border

Well-manicured formal lawn

Range of colourful summer-flowering bedding plants

Firm, all-weather surface formed of paving slabs

Second herbaceous border complementing the other

Lawn and bedding plants mirroring the opposite side

Central brick path

RANGE OF PLANTS

Using a wide range of plants creates greater interest.

- **Hardy annuals:** these are sown in their flowering position outdoors in spring; they die in autumn.

- **Half-hardy annuals:** these are sown in gentle warmth in late winter or early spring and planted in early summer; they die in autumn.

- **Herbaceous perennials:** these grow and flower for 3–4 years before being lifted and divided. Each year, plants die down to ground level in autumn and develop fresh shoots in spring.

- **Bulbs, corms and tubers:** there is a wide range of types, but all are powerhouses of stored energy. Some flower in winter or spring, others in summer or autumn.

- **Climbers:** a few of these are hardy annuals, while others are perennial and will grow happily from one year to another with very little attention.

- **Shrubs:** these are woody-natured, with several stems growing from ground level. Most live for ten years or more. They can be deciduous or evergreen.

- **Small trees:** these are woody-natured, with a single stem (trunk) connecting the branches to the roots. Most live for 20 or more years, and they can be deciduous or evergreen.

Honeysuckle arbour

As well as clothing porches and rustic arches alongside boundary hedges and over garden paths, consider creating a Honeysuckle-clothed arbour in a secluded part of your garden. Such a feature has a relaxed character and is best used in an informal setting. Choose a semi-rustic bench.

INITIAL COST

- With shrubs, the initial cost is high, but remember that this will be spread over ten years or more.
- Herbaceous perennials are less expensive than shrubs, and they can be lifted and divided after 3–4 years before being replanted, thus creating more plants for free.
- Summer-flowering bedding plants have a summer-only value, but displays can be changed each season.

MAINTENANCE TIME

Keeping a herbaceous border tidy throughout summer requires more attention than just a border full of shrubs and underplanted with bulbs. Summer-flowering bedding plants also need regular care, including pulling out weeds, watering and removing dead flowers and invasive stems.

Informal gardens

How can I create a restful ambience?

Informality in gardens appeals to many home gardeners and especially to devotees of a relaxed, casual and Bohemian way of life. Traditionally, cottage gardens had this feel, where plants of all types jostled side by side in the same bed. Fortunately, even in small gardens this ambience can be recreated through informal plants and features, as well as decorative and relaxed paths, fences and hedges. Remember, also, to choose rustic benches.

Planned informality is the key to achieving a successful look with relaxed and informal gardens.

SOOTHING SOUNDS?

As well as demure colours and irregular shapes, soothing sounds have a relaxing nature. These range from the rustling of leaves to the reassuring pitter-patter of water splashing and tumbling from fountains and waterfalls.

A few bamboos are ideal for planting in a small garden and these are described on page 50, as well as their use in Mediterranean and Japanese gardens on pages 24–25. Their leaves rustle in even the slightest breeze, creating a soothing and irregular sound. Additionally, some can be grown in containers, and these are ideal for bringing both colour and sound closer to a house.

Garden wind chimes suspended from trees and close to a house create gentle and comforting sounds, but do not position them where they are easily knocked.

INFORMAL LAYOUT EXAMPLES

Brick paths crossing an area of shingle create texture variations

Irregularly positioned paving slabs create an unusual, attractive path

Natural stone paths epitomize a relaxed and informal garden

Meandering, maze-like paths have eye appeal, especially for children

Curved patios and paths create a unified, informal garden

A meandering path, combined with shrubs, creates mystery in a garden

RELAXED LAYOUT AND INFORMAL PLANTS

Several examples of informal designs are featured on the left of this page. Remember to ensure that paths, lawn edges and borders do not create straight lines, and check that garden furniture completes the informality. Rustic benches and thin-framed metal chairs have a relaxed nature.

Wisteria sinensis 'Alba', with its clusters of attractive white flowers, contrasts well with the old brick wall behind it.

DESIGN FOR AN INFORMAL GARDEN

Although small and informal, a garden must have a focal point. There are several to consider, including:

- Benches constructed with a framework of thin, rustic poles but with a flat sitting area.
- Wrought-iron chairs and tables, perhaps with the benefit of lighting.
- Bird baths and tables positioned on an informally paved area – but always make sure uneaten food does not attract squirrels.
- Armillary spheres and informal statues – use these to create relaxed focal points.
- Grass benches surrounded by clipped Box – these are simple to construct and ideal for a relaxed area at the end of an informal path.

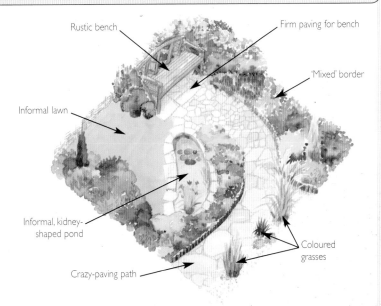

Rustic bench

Firm paving for bench

'Mixed' border

Informal lawn

Informal, kidney-shaped pond

Coloured grasses

Crazy-paving path

INFORMAL PATHS

↗ *Ideas for informal paths include well-weathered bricks (not concrete pavers), sections of logs, reconstituted stone, and circular pavers (see above) that can be laid to create an attractive and unusual meandering path.*

↗ *Natural stone with small, prostrate plants positioned between them creates a cottage-garden ambience. An alternative is crazy paving, which is not quite so informal.*

INFORMAL BACKGROUNDS

Stone wall with built-in plant shelves

Wattle fencing has a countrified appearance

Natural stone walls are informal in appearance, but are available to only a few home gardeners. There are some other relaxed, and much cheaper, backgrounds, including the following.

- **Wattle panels:** ideal for a 'countrified' fence, but they do not create a strong barrier against animals.
- **Interwoven panels:** these create a solid screen, usually in panels 1.8 m (6 ft) long and in several heights.
- **Horizontal lap panels:** overlapping horizontal strips are attached to a framework, and are sold in panels 1.8 m (6 ft) wide and in several heights.

GAZEBOS AND ORNAMENTAL WELLS

Gazebos are distinctive features and certain to gain attention, as well as forming leisure areas. By definition, they allow people to 'gaze out' onto a garden. They have a long history, originating in early Persian gardens, and generally have a wooden framework, with wooden lattice-work at the back and an ornate roof. An ornamental well is sure to attract glances; but you must ensure that it has a firm surround.

Ornamental wells need strong construction

Rustic gazebos have a informal nature

INFORMAL FURNITURE

This wooden chair is casual in character

Stone benches can be used to display plants

In addition to the examples of informal furniture discussed above as focal points (see top left), there are others:

- ✔ **Stone benches** formed of reconstituted stone have a relaxed look. Be prepared in spring to remove algae – use a soft brush and soapy water.
- ✔ **Collapsible chairs** (both metal and wood) are available in several designs. Store them in a shed during winter.

Formal gardens

Are formal gardens time-consuming?

Regimented gardens must be kept neat and tidy, otherwise they will lose their distinctive character. Neatly outlined edges of *Buxus sempervirens* 'Suffruticosa' (Dwarf Edging Box) need to be maintained throughout the year, while edgings of formal summer-flowering bedding plants require attention to ensure that they do not invade each other or become dominated by weeds. Lawns require regular mowing and edge trimming.

CLASSICAL HERITAGE

Creating patterns and shapes has long captivated gardeners, usually by using plants such as trees and shrubs to produce permanent designs. Seasonal patterns in gardens have also been created, mainly using summer-flowering annuals in neat designs popularized through 'carpet bedding' (also known as tapestry, mosaic and jewel bedding) in the 1800s. It gained an enthusiastic following, with motifs and intricate patterns created in local and national competitions.

Shapes and patterns are claimed to influence our lives and to have curative values. However, not everyone is sensitive to the auras created by pattern therapy, described in writings dating back several thousand years. Nevertheless, plants in attractive patterns seldom fail to attract attention.

Formal bedding schemes – earlier and still widely known as carpet bedding.

FORMAL LAYOUTS AND PLANTING EXAMPLES

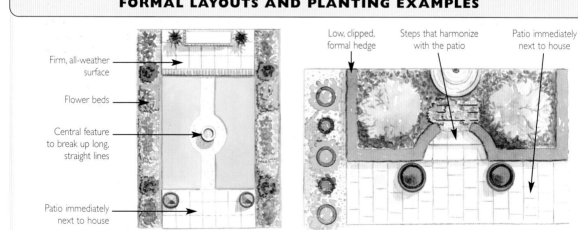

Firm, all-weather surface

Flower beds

Central feature to break up long, straight lines

Patio immediately next to house

Low, clipped, formal hedge

Steps that harmonize with the patio

Patio immediately next to house

↗ *This design exudes formality, with rigid lines that soon take the eye right to the end of the garden, where an additional leisure area has been created.*

↗ *Where a formal garden is to be on a slope, first construct a patio area next to the house and then create a series of steps. A small hedge will help to unify the design.*

Plants for formal summer bedding

Here are a few of the most popular plants used in summer bedding.

- *Begonia semperflorens* (Fibrous-rooted Begonia/Wax Begonia): tender perennial invariably grown as a half-hardy annual. Glossy green or purple leaves are surmounted from early to late summer by red, pink or white flowers.
Height: 15–23 cm (6–9 in) Spread: 20–25 cm (8–10 in)

- *Lobelia erinus* (Edging Lobelia): half-hardy perennial invariably grown as a half-hardy annual. Masses of blue, white or red flowers throughout summer. Some forms have trailing stems and are best used in hanging-baskets.
Height: 10–23 cm (4–9 in) Spread: 10–15 cm (4–6 in)

- *Lobularia maritima* (Sweet Alyssum; also known as *Alyssum maritimum*): hardy annual usually grown as a half-hardy annual. Densely covered with rounded clusters of white, violet-purple, rose-carmine or deep purple flowers throughout summer.
Height: 7.5–15 cm (3–6 in) Spread: 20–30 cm (8–12 in)

- *Salvia splendens* (Scarlet Salvia): tender perennial invariably grown as a half-hardy annual. Glossy green leaves are surmounted from early to late summer by red, pink or white flowers.
Height: 30–38 cm (12–15 in) Spread: 23–38 cm (9–15 in)

- *Tanacetum parthenium* 'Aureum' (Edging Chrysanthemum; also known as *Chrysanthemum parthenium* 'Aureum'): short-lived perennial raised as a half-hardy annual. It produces aromatic, light green leaves and white flowers from mid-summer to early autumn.
Height: 23–30 cm (9–12 in) Spread: 20–25 cm (8–10 in)

DOT PLANTS FOR SUMMER FLOWERING

- *Abutilon pictum* 'Thompsonii' (Flowering Maple; also known as *Abutilon striatum* 'Thompsonii'): half-hardy perennial with maple-like, dark green leaves splashed and spotted in bright yellow.
Height: 90 cm–1.2 m (3–4 ft)
Spread: 38–45 cm (15–18 in)

- *Bassia scoparia* 'Childsii' (also known as *Kochia scoparia* 'Childsii'): half-hardy annual. Light green foliage. Height: 45 cm (1½ ft)
Spread: 23–30 cm (9–12 in)

- *Canna* x *generalis* (Indian Shot): half-hardy perennial. There are two main types – green-leaved and purple- or brown-leaved.
Height: 75 cm–1 m (2½–3½ ft)
Spread: 30–38 cm (12–15 in)

- *Cordyline australis* (Cabbage Palm): slow-growing and tender evergreen.
Height: 60–90 cm (3–4 ft)
Spread: 45 cm (1½ ft)

FORMAL FEATURES

Paths and steps

Use colour- and shape-harmonizing materials   *Ensure the path's edges are strong and firm*

⬆ Straight paths and steps, perhaps formed of clinically arranged paving slabs or concrete pavers, epitomize the nature of a formal path.

Decorative screens

This decorative screen has an open character   *Varied-height screens create greater interest*

⬆ Ornamental screens and entrances have an attractive yet functional nature, helping to create distinctive and separate parts in a garden.

Porches

Attractive porches always enhance a house   *Even a small porch adds distinction*

⬆ Porches constructed from planed timber and with a tiled or boarded roof create formality. They can be attached to a formal-style fence.

Pergolas

Radial-topped pergolas are distinctive   *You can fit seats into corner-type structures*

⬆ Pergola-type structures need not be solely positioned over a path. A small, hard-surfaced area is enhanced by overhead screening.

Lawn centrepieces

Sundials are popular in open areas   *Bird baths should have a shallow basin*

⬆ Clinically outlined lawn features, such as bird baths and sundials. On a small lawn, keep their size in proportion to the area, ensuring they are not dominant.

Water features

Wall-mounted fountains are very decorative   *Pebble fountains are safe for children*

⬆ Several types of water feature can be integrated into a small garden. Try a small fountain against a wall, or create a pebble pond.

Mediterranean influences

Can I evoke Mediterranean memories?

Many people, when remembering the relaxed and idyllic nature of a Mediterranean holiday, would like to recreate the atmosphere in their own garden – whatever its size. Sun-loving plants in pots can be grouped on even the smallest patio, while a small water-garden feature, with perhaps a repetitive sound, adds a relaxing note to the scene. However, it is essential that the area you choose has sun for much of the day, especially in the evenings.

PERFECT FOR A SMALL SPACE

A small, cloistered area is ideal for a Mediterranean garden. When walls partly enclose the site, paint them white to reflect as much light as possible. This extra light benefits the growth of plants and remember that flower colours such as yellow, gold, red, scarlet and dark blue are especially noticeable against a white background. Alternatively, grey-stone walls enhance and highlight pinks, reds, deep blues and purples.

PAVED AREAS FOR TABLES AND CHAIRS

A level, paved area is essential for a table and several chairs. For the creation of a Mediterranean aura, choose metal-structured furniture rather than anything with a heavy, thick and rustic nature. White or light-coloured tops to tables help to reflect light and to create an open feel.

The herbaceous Nepeta x faassenii *(Catmint) creates a Mediterranean look.*

CONSERVING MOISTURE

When establishing plants in a hot, Mediterranean-type garden, conserving moisture in the soil is important. Here are a couple of ways in which to do this:

- After planting, form a 2.5 cm (1 in) thick mulch of stones over the surface. This reduces moisture-loss from the soil and keep the roots cool.

- If natural stone slabs are used to create an informal patio, extend them over the roots.

OVERHEAD SHADE FROM CLIMBERS

In hot areas, strong sunlight can make a small garden inhospitable for part of the day. Therefore, an overhead canopy formed by leafy climbers is welcome. Many climbers are illustrated and described on page 47, but you could also consider a grapevine. For a distinctive and decorative Mediterranean-type canopy and screen, try *Vitis vinifera* 'Purpurea' (Teinturier Grape), which has claret-red leaves that in autumn turn rich purple before falling.

FRAGRANT LILIES IN POTS

The range of Lilies is wide, and fragrant ones for growing in pots on a warm patio include:
- *Lilium longiflorum* (**Easter Lily**): white, trumpet-shaped flowers with golden pollen and a honey-like scent during mid- and late summer.
- *Lilium auratum* (**Golden-rayed Lily**): fragrant, bowl-shaped, white flowers with a golden-yellow ray or band and purple coloured spots on the inner surface of each petal in late summer and early autumn.

MEDITERRANEAN GARDEN PLANTS

Silver-leaved shrubs thrive in warm climates and three that will remind you of warm, heady and restful evenings include:
- *Artemisia abrotanum* (**Southernwood/Lad's Love**): bushy shrub, with a deciduous or semi-evergreen nature and aromatic, grey leaves.
- *Artemisia arborescens*: deciduous or semi-evergreen, tender shrub with silvery-white leaves and round, yellow flowers that are produced during early and mid-summer.
- *Santolina chamaecyparissus* (**Cotton Lavender**): forms a mound of finely divided, silvery, woolly leaves. Bright yellow flowers appear during mid-summer.

Plants in pots

Scented-leaved Pelargoniums have a warm-climate nature and in temperate climates can be put outdoors in pots during summer; they need protection in winter. The range of leaf fragrances is wide, including:

Use several different types of plants

Pelargonium crispum (Lemon Geranium) has lemon-scented leaves and pink flowers.

Pelargonium graveolens (Rose Geranium) has sweet and rose-scented leaves, and rose-pink flowers with dark purple spots.

Pelargonium tomentosum (Mint Geranium) produces peppermint-scented leaves and white flowers.

Group together different sized and shaped pots

Japanese influences

Japanese gardens exude peace, serenity and contemplation and have a distinctive, uncluttered character that encourages meditation and a desire to know oneself. The design of Japanese gardens is an expression of appreciation and delight in the beauty of nature, which must be respected. Water features and decorated bridges, plants in containers and a gravel base combine to produce a distinctive garden that creates interest throughout the year.

Can I have a meditative garden?

Areas of gravel, incorporating a stepping-stone path, create a perfect base for a Japanese garden.

SERENITY

A thousand years ago countryside noises were clearly heard, and the loudest sound was often the ringing of church bells. Nowadays the intrusion of general noise has almost removed this cherished, life-calming quality, something which a Japanese garden attempts to recapture.

MINIMALISM

A Japanese garden is one that is in balance with nature, where neither plants nor structural introductions dominate each other. An uncluttered background is essential and this can be achieved by erecting a bamboo-like screen.

GRAVEL

Few parts of a Japanese garden are as restful to the eye as gravel, which can be given extra interest by laying a stepping stone path across it, but avoid splitting it up and producing two unrelated areas. Raking the surface of gravel creates the impression of water and waves.

BAMBOOS FOR CONTAINERS

Bamboos, with their distinctive quality, are essential parts of Japanese gardens and several are suitable for growing in containers, including:
- *Fargesia nitida*: a hardy and evergreen bamboo, with bright green leaves and light purple canes.
- *Phyllostachys nigra*: dark green leaves and canes first green, later jet-black.
- *Pleioblastus viridistriatus*: purple-green canes and golden-yellow leaves with pea-green stripes.

OTHER PLANTS FOR CONTAINERS

- *Acer palmatum* var. *dissectum* 'Atropurpureum': hardy, slow-growing, deciduous, dome-headed tree with finely dissected, bronze-red leaves.
- *Acer palmatum* var. *dissectum*: as above, but with all-green leaves.
- *Fatsia japonica*: this is the False Castor Oil Plant, evergreen and slightly tender with large, glossy, hand-like leaves.

OUTDOOR BONSAI

Bonsai has a natural affinity with Japanese gardens, where the art of growing diminutive trees and shrubs in shallow containers was refined. Today, the art of bonsai has spread to many other countries. Bonsai can be displayed on staging, as well as on 'monkey poles', which have flat tops and are available at different heights so that a bonsai can be easily admired by everyone.

Tea garden

A garden is an essential part of a tea ceremony. In a tranquil setting, those taking part first assemble to cast off worldly cares. Trees, shrubs and ferns, with their perennial nature, create a timeless aura. Ephemeral flowers, however, are not allowed, as they express the passing of time.

Feng shui

Originally in Chinese mythology but known in Japanese culture, feng shui is a concept of spirit influences – good and evil – which inhabit natural features in landscapes. By orientating plants and entrances, spirits are given the opportunity to enter and depart.

INITIAL COST

The cost of creating a Japanese garden on a large scale is prohibitive, but it is an ideal feature for a small garden, when costs are more realistic and less painful. Some garden views, especially those that are very drab or seen out of basement flat windows, can be radically improved with a wide range of planted and container-grown plants.

Container gardening

Growing plants in containers has never been more popular, and many home gardeners find it an ideal way to grow plants in a small garden, especially when courtyard, patio and balcony gardening are the only opportunities. A wide range of containers – from hanging-baskets to tubs and pots – is described below. Additionally, some gardeners rely on containers such as wall-baskets, mangers, windowboxes and wall-secured pots to create colour.

Is it easy in a small garden?

Short, bushy, summer-flowering bedding plants are superb for bringing eye-catching colour to containers.

Wall-baskets can be used to drench walls with welcome colour, especially in combination with hanging-baskets.

Hanging-baskets create colour at about head height. Ensure, however, that they cannot be knocked.

CONTAINERS CREATE MORE SPACE

Containers suspended from wall-secured brackets or supported on windowsills leave more space at ground level for larger and often more permanent plants in tubs and pots, where a firm base is essential. To get the best displays, however, try permutations of them all.

CONTAINERS BECOME PART OF THE INFRASTRUCTURE

In small gardens, tubs and large pots planted with shrubs, trees and conifers become permanent parts of a garden. These containers can be displayed in many positions – near to doors, either side of a window or in a corner on a patio. Ephemeral plants in pots and troughs can be temporarily placed around them during summer, where they gain protection from wind and strong sunlight. Alpines and miniature rock-garden plants in old stone sinks last several years.

RANGE OF CONTAINERS

Pots and tubs

← From wooden tubs to terracotta pots. Make sure that they harmonize with their surroundings.

Old stone sinks

← Old stone sinks can be used as miniature water gardens, as well as for rock-garden plants.

Windowboxes

← These are ideal for clothing both sash and casement windows in colour.

Hanging-baskets

← Position these at head height, between windows or either side of a doorway.

Wall-baskets and mangers

← These help bare walls between windows, and around entrances, to become awash with colour.

Old artefacts

← You will be surprised at how many old pieces of 'jumble' can be used to create unusual plant holders.

DECORATING SMALL PATIOS AND COURTYARDS

It is best to choose a combination of floor-positioned pots and tubs and hanging-baskets and windowboxes.

- Where space is severely limited, use mainly wall-mounted displays as well as windowboxes.
- Try to direct foot traffic away from open casement windows by using tubs and large pots of shrubs and upright conifers in appropriate positions. Sink gardens will also guide foot traffic.
- Position troughs packed with culinary herbs near a kitchen door.

Roof gardens and balconies

Weather-resistant displays are essential for roof gardens. Balconies create a more plant-friendly environment, although even they can be blustery and cold if facing away from the sun (there is more information on page 29).

DOORWAY AND STEP DISPLAYS

Brightly decorated entrances and steps give immediate vitality and interest to houses and flats. Position a series of colour-packed pots alongside stepped entrances – and, if space allows, on the steps.

LOOKING AFTER CONTAINER PLANTS

Accessibility is the main consideration when you are looking after container-grown plants in a courtyard, basement, entrance or on a patio. Always use a reliable stepladder when watering plants that are raised up high. Alternatively, use a proprietary watering device that enables watering to be carried out from ground level. There is also the possibility of making a home-made watering device; to do this, tie the end of a hosepipe to a long bamboo cane.

USING A WALL AS A GARDEN

→ At first sight, an old wall in a small courtyard or basement entrance may appear to be inhospitable, but it is amazing how wall gardening can transform it. Tiered troughs, wall-baskets, mangers and windowboxes all create attractive homes for plants.

TROUGHS

Large troughs positioned at ground level become homes for many plants, including small or slow-growing conifers. Choose conifers with different colours and shapes. These displays can be left in position for several years.

PLANTING POCKETS

Recessed areas in walls are novel places for small pots packed with upright or trailing plants. Where recesses are alongside a flight of steps, make sure pots cannot be knocked and toppled. They will require frequent watering during hot weather.

Choosing plants for different containers

Suitable plants for container gardening in a small area depends on the nature of the container. Here are some clues to their success.

Pots ~ choose from summer-flowering annuals to scented-leaved Geraniums (botanically, Pelargoniums). Ensure that pots cannot be toppled, especially if they have a large proportion of foliage.

Tubs ~ these are ideal for woody perennials such as shrubs, trees and conifers. They will need a permanent position on a patio, terrace or courtyard.

Windowboxes ~ these never fail to create interest, with displays specially selected for spring, summer, and winter. Those that create summer displays rely mainly on summer-flowering bedding plants; displays in winter are frequently devoted to dwarf conifers and small, hardy, bushy and trailing evergreen shrubs;

spring displays are packed with spring-flowering bulbs and hardy, bushy and trailing evergreen shrubs.

Hanging-baskets ~ these are ideal for creating colour at head height, and with their summer-only display are packed with bushy, trailing and cascading, summer-flowering bedding plants. Trailing and cascading plants such as Fuchsias are also used.

Wall-baskets ~ these resemble hanging-baskets cut in half and secured to a wall. During summer they become awash with bushy and trailing summer-flowering bedding plants, and in spring with bulbs and biennials.

Mangers ~ these are similar to wall-baskets, but are made with thicker and more substantial metal, and are usually wider, creating dominant features. Plant in the same way as for wall-baskets.

Wild gardens

Are they possible in a small area?

Wild gardens are not a contradiction in terms, but a planned and fascinating way of introducing wild landscape features into a garden, whatever its size. Additionally, this approach is good for the environment. Too often, fields are intensively cultivated, hedges removed and long grass and native plants cut down. Yet even a small wildlife area in a garden, perhaps with a diminutive pond, helps redress this negative attitude towards the environment.

WILDLIFE GARDENS

These are best given a quiet, out-of-the-way position, but one where the feature and activities of its residents can be readily seen. Such tranquillity brings pleasure to many gardeners and can be cathartic. A light, overhead canopy provided by deciduous trees helps to create shade for ground-level plants, birds and small mammals. It also keeps the soil damp and cool during

Wildlife areas introduce a new dimension to gardening.

summer, a benefit to many insects as well as small mammals. Where a pond is part of the feature, in autumn you will need to scoop out dead leaves that have fallen from trees.

Frogs and toads are beneficial in gardens

Dragonflies are attracted by water

Newts are attractive creatures in ponds

WILDFLOWER GARDENS

After many years of plant breeding and creating new varieties, many gardeners realize that native plants have a grace, charm and delicacy not present in human-created forms. Native wildflowers usually have an annual or perennial nature; both create magnificent displays. Wildflowers also attract a wide range of insects, including butterflies. Many seed companies sell individual wildflower species, as well as mixtures. They are best sown in spring and, while annuals reseed themselves each year, perennials become permanently established – although even they produce seed that germinates in suitable conditions.

HOW TO SOW

During early winter, fork or dig the soil, loosening the surface to about 20 cm (8 in) deep. Leave the surface uneven but approximately level; in late winter or early spring, rake the area and systematically shuffle over it to create a moderately firm surface. In mid- and late spring, thinly scatter seeds over the surface and lightly cover them by using a rake. Gently but thoroughly water the area, taking care not to wash away the seeds by mistake.

WILDLIFE PONDS

Unlike ornamental garden ponds, wildlife types are meant to be havens for birds, amphibians, insects and small mammals, as well as fish. Aquatic plants, together with those along the edges, create retreats for insects.

BOG GARDENS

These are often linked with water features, and are where moisture-loving plants can be grown. Because of their leafy and informal nature they also attract insects and small mammals.

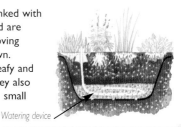

Watering device

Fragrant flowers

Some seed companies sell mixtures of fragrant annuals. These are not necessarily wildflowers, but can still be raised in the same way as suggested for wildflowers (see left). Mixtures of fragrant perennials are also available.

Protecting garden wildlife

When encouraging wildlife into your garden, do not use insecticides or weedkillers. Contaminated flowers and leaves are deadly to fish, amphibians, insects and small mammals.

Balcony and roof gardening

It is surprising how much colour can be created on a balcony or roof, whatever its aspect. Pots, troughs and hanging-baskets packed with summer-flowering bedding plants are ideal during summer, while from autumn to spring reliance is mainly on small, evergreen shrubs and dwarf conifers. When tender plants are grown, these may have to be taken indoors during winter. Alternatively, a friend with a frost-proof greenhouse might be able to offer them sanctuary.

Is balcony or roof gardening practical?

Roof gardens are idyllic throughout summer; perennial plants in containers can be removed during winter to a less exposed position.

ON TOP OF THE WORLD

Roof gardens are popular where the climate allows more than half the year to be spent on it. In other places, despite initial enthusiasm, the reality of a seasonal garden becomes apparent when icy winds roar across the site. Conversely, during summer the area may be exposed to strong, scorching sunlight, which may be ideal when attempting to gain an attractive sun tan but will shrivel plants which are not regularly watered. Nevertheless, the ability to garden 'on top of the world' has unmatched eye appeal.

ROOF-GARDEN IDEAS

Construct screens to create privacy as well as giving you protection from strong wind. In summer, temporary privacy screens may be all that is needed. Privacy screens are also essential to reassure neighbours they are not being spied upon; before problems arise, tell them about your plans.

In windy positions, it is best to rely on summer-flowering plants in troughs and tubs to create colour.

Construct a series of strong railings along the outer edges of the roof garden and then train small-leaved, variegated Ivies to grow over them.

Balcony key features

In cold and exposed areas rely mainly on summer displays from summer-flowering bedding plants. Use trailing, small-leaved, variegated Ivies to create more permanent colour.

Roof-garden caution

Check that the infrastructure is suitable (see page 9) and there is an easily accessible source of water. A combination of strong sunlight and breezes soon causes compost to become dry.

MAKING THE MOST OF A BALCONY

- For a colour contrast, secure pots of red or scarlet Geraniums (Pelargoniums) to the tops of white railings. At floor level, use a combination of trailing *Lysimachia nummularia* 'Aurea' (yellow flowers and leaves) and red Petunias. Let the *Lysimachia* trail through the railings.

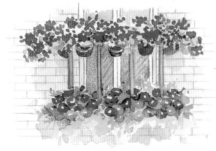

- Fragrant displays in spring can be created from troughs or large pots of *Hyacinthus orientalis* (Hyacinths), in colours including white, rose-pink and soft blue. Plant them in autumn and await a magnificent, superbly fragrant display the following year.
- Several Lilies can be grown in pots on warm and wind-sheltered balconies – see page 24 for fragrant types.

LEISURE BALCONIES

In addition to growing plants on balconies, don't forget that they are leisure areas:

- Where the view allows and the balcony's size is suitable, consider having a deck-chair and small table that can both be easily stored indoors when not in use.

- Low-intensity and unobtrusive lights provide another opportunity for making the best of a balcony after the sun has gone down.

Creating a secluded garden

Is privacy important in a garden?

Areas within a garden that offer seclusion and privacy are highly prized. They become oases of calm and contemplation, where sanity can be reclaimed. In large gardens many places offer natural privacy, but in small gardens it has to be created, perhaps by the construction of arbours, trellises and pergolas, then cloaking these with floriferous and fragrant climbers. Buying or constructing a gazebo or summerhouse are other possibilities.

WAYS TO CREATE PRIVACY

- **Erect a free-standing trellis** about 45 cm (18 in) from a boundary and cloak it with leafy and floriferous climbers such as *Clematis montana*.
- **Construct an arbour** with crossbeams at its top and plant a grapevine to create a Mediterranean feature. Several forms have ornamental foliage, such as *Vitis vinifera* 'Purpurea' (claret-red leaves when young, becoming vinous-purple).
- **Decorative fences**, such as wattle screens, create a cottage garden aura and help to provide privacy. More formal types are better for modern gardens.
- **Ready-made arbours, arches and pergolas** are available from garden centres and through mail-order catalogues for rapid construction.

ROMANTIC ARBOURS

Few gardeners can resist the opportunity to create a romantic arbour, cloaked in leafy plants as well as flowers – and drenched in rich fragrances. Here are some romantic climbers to consider.
- *Clematis montana* **(Mountain Clematis):** pure white flowers in late spring and into early summer. 'Elizabeth' has soft pink, slightly fragrant flowers, while 'Alexander' is creamy-white and with a stronger scent.
- *Lonicera periclymenum* **'Belgica' (Early Dutch Honeysuckle):** purple-red and yellow, sweetly fragrant flowers during late spring and early summer.
- *Lonicera periclymenum* **'Serotina' (Late Dutch Honeysuckle):** flowers reddish-purple on the inside and creamy-white on the outside, from mid-summer to autumn. Sweetly fragrant.

SCREENING OFF NEIGHBOURS

Here are a few solutions to prevent neighbours seeing into your garden, whether they are looking in at ground height or from upstairs windows.

Close-boarded fencing produces an attractive peep-proof screen.

Small, ready-made ornate arbours can be fitted into a garden of any size.

Decorative wooden fencing and lattice screens can look stunning.

Insert projecting bricks into walls so they can be used to hold plant pots.

Open-fronted, lean-to constructions are inexpensive and make suitable homes for container plants.

An overhead framework can be covered with decorative flowering and leafy climbers.

Unusual planting ideas for privacy

It may be possible to construct features farther into your garden and away from nearby houses, so don't just create privacy immediately around your house.

Paths with arches over them and planted with leafy and flowering climbers, or, for something different, a tunnel (see page 73).

If your garden faces the sun, position a summerhouse with its back to the house and front facing down the garden. Erect a lattice-work or rustic screen on the side facing the house to make it more attractive.

Erect strong bean poles and form a screen of runner beans. You will be surprised how attractive they are as well as enjoying the bonus of your own fresh vegetables to eat.

HEDGE FACTS

- **Hedges are a living part** of gardens and therefore quickly harmonize with other plants.
- **Hedges filter wind** rather than totally block it. They therefore do not create turbulent eddies on their leeward side.
- **Hedges impoverish soil** around their base, as well as keeping it dry.
- **Plant hedges at least** half their expected width from a boundary to prevent shoots later trespassing on neighbouring properties.
- **Many hedges need regular clipping** – at least three or four times a year.
- **Hedges create shade**, which may annoy neighbours.
- **Some hedges are low and easily maintained;** others are too vigorous for small gardens.

Low-maintenance gardens

There are subtle differences between 'low' and 'easy' maintenance, although the reasoning is often blurred. An easy-maintenance garden is a lawn – and little else. All that is needed is to cut the grass weekly, from spring to autumn. This design is ideal for young families, where ball games and bicycles take priority. A low-maintenance garden is one where the area is planned to have desirable features and plants, yet require minimal maintenance.

Low maintenance or easy maintenance?

LOW-MAINTENANCE PLANTS

Once established, many plants create magnificent displays and with minimal attention. Here are some to consider:

- **Herbaceous perennials:** some are self-supporting and trouble-free (see pages 38–41).
- **Ground-cover plants:** plants that smother the soil's surface with attractive leaves and flowers that prevent the growth of weeds.
- **Naturalized bulbs:** large-faced Daffodils

planted in out-of-the-way grassy areas will produce magnificent displays in spring. Once flowering is over, leave the foliage to wither and die naturally.

- **Shrubs and small trees:** both deciduous and evergreen types are low-maintenance plants. Apart from a little (or no) pruning, shrubs and small trees need minimal attention once established. For some low-maintenance shrubs and trees, see pages 42–45.

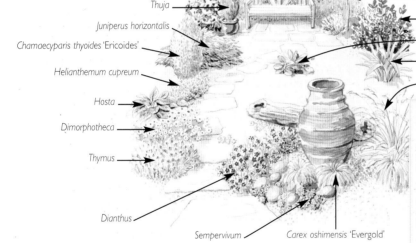

Thuja

Juniperus horizontalis

Chamaecyparis thyoides 'Ericoides'

Helianthemum cupreum

Hosta

Dimorphotheca

Thymus

Dianthus

Sempervivum

Carex oshimensis 'Evergold'

Sorbus aria 'Lutescens'

Photinia x fraseri

Bergenia cordifolia

Phormium

Stipa calamagrostis

EQUIPMENT FOR EASY GARDENING

Mechanical equipment has taken the physical toil out of gardening and made it an even greater pleasure.

Electric lawn mowers: ideal for gardeners who need to have regular rests when mowing (the machine can be easily stopped and it is then silent).

Petrol-powered lawn mowers: excellent for large lawns or where a safe electrical supply is not available.

Strimmers: suitable for cutting long grass or clearing undergrowth. Some models convert to trim lawn edges.

Hedge trimmers: make hedge cutting less arduous than with manual shears.

Lawn rakes: take the strain out of raking, sweeping and scarifying lawns.

Compost shredders: used to convert woody garden waste into invaluable mulch to protect the garden soil.

GARDEN TOOL SAFETY: Don't neglect safety (see page 13).

Design factors for easy gardening

When designing garden features, think about the mechanical equipment used with them.

Alongside border edges, and especially where herbaceous perennials spread over the edge of a lawn and create bare areas, install a row of 45 cm (18 in) square paving slabs. Plants can then be allowed to spread and soften unattractive border edges, while a hover mower can be used to cut up to and slightly over the edging.

Where stepping stones are inset into lawns, check that they are set

fractionally below the lawn surface so that, without damage, a hover mower can be used to cut the grass.

Where lawns abut walls, install a cutting strip to enable edges to be cut without damaging the mower or grazing hands against the brickwork.

Where lawn edges are alongside borders, use a half-moon edging iron to cut each edge or long-arm edging shears to trim them. For this edging type, cut the grass with a cylinder-type mower with a roller, rather than a hover mower.

Food-producing gardens

Is this possible in a small garden?

Whatever the size of a small garden, it is possible to grow vegetables and fruit. Fertile patches in gardens create opportunities for rows of salad vegetables, while pots, tubs and growing-bags offer space-saving homes for many others, including culinary herbs. Apples can be grown in tubs and large pots on a patio. Strawberries are suitable for planters and hanging-baskets; tomatoes can also be planted in hanging-baskets.

WHAT TO EXPECT FROM A SMALL GARDEN

Small vegetable patches are ideal for salad-type crops, such as lettuces, carrots, spring onions, beetroot and tomatoes. French beans, with their low, bush-type habit, are another possibility. Vegetables with a perennial nature, such as asparagus and globe artichokes, are best left for larger gardens.

Potatoes in small gardens are usually treated as a novelty crop and grown in tubs, large pots or proprietary potato-growing containers. Additionally, they can be grown in peat-based compost in black plastic bags.

Apples grown as cordons or espaliers against walls make full use of space; in tubs and large pots they have a shorter life-span.

VEGETABLES IN WINDOWBOXES

Regular watering is essential to stop plants wilting and the crops being damaged.
- **Cucumbers:** plant compact varieties as soon as plants are available and all risk of frost has passed. Pinch out the growing point when the plant has 6–7 leaves.
- **Sweet peppers:** when all risk of frost has passed, put 2–3 young plants in a windowbox. Harvest then when the fruits are swollen and glossy.
- **Tomatoes:** plant two bush-type tomato plants as soon as all risk of frost has passed. It is not necessary to remove sideshoots.

Wigwams formed of bamboo canes soon become drenched in leaves and beans.

VEGETABLE GARDEN DESIGN

Small-garden vegetable plots need not be formal, with plants growing in clinical rows at right-angles to paths. Climbing beans are ideal for scaling trellises and bamboo wigwams, while a half-standard Bay tree creates distinction in a herb area.

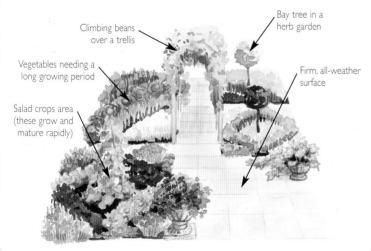

Climbing beans over a trellis

Vegetables needing a long growing period

Salad crops area (these grow and mature rapidly)

Bay tree in a herb garden

Firm, all-weather surface

TOMATOES IN SMALL GREENHOUSES

Even the smallest greenhouse offers gardening opportunities, especially for tomatoes. Plant a standard-sized growing-bag with 3–4 cordon-type plants; support them either with canes pushed through the bag and into the soil, or with a proprietary supporting frame.

Vegetables for growing-bags

Here are four popular vegetables to try.

Bush French beans ~ grow six plants in each bag.

Courgettes ~ two plants in a bag.

Lettuces ~ eight lettuces in a bag.

Tomatoes ~ see above.

HERBS IN TINY PLACES

Where space is limited, try growing herbs in a cartwheel pattern – it is both decorative and practical.

- Prepare soil in winter, digging and removing perennial weeds. Rake the soil level in spring.
- Use large pebbles to form a circle 1.5–1.8 m (5–6 ft) wide. Add a central circle and spokes.
- Plant a dominant herb in the centre (perhaps a Bay tree).
- Plant different herbs in the areas between the spokes.
- Spread shingle or coloured gravel around the plants and between the spokes. This helps to conserve moisture in the soil.

Strawberries in containers

Containers to try:

Planters with cupped holes in their sides ~ leave plants in the container for 2–3 years.

Hanging-baskets ~ use three plants in a large basket.

Windowboxes and wall-baskets ~ space plants about 20 cm (8 in) apart.

Barrels with holes cut in their sides ~ put one plant in each hole, as well as several in the top.

TREE FRUITS

The three tree fruits most popular with home gardeners for growing against walls or alongside paths are:

- **Apples:** use dwarfing rootstocks such as M27 and M9, and choose a space-saving form (see below). Additionally, choose varieties not readily available in shops.
- **Pears:** use the Quince A rootstock, and train trees as espaliers or cordons. Pears need pollination partners, so grow three different varieties as cordons, such as 'Conference', 'Doyenne du Comice' and 'Williams' Bon Chrétien'.
- **Peaches and nectarines:** use St Julien A rootstock, and grow as a fan.

SPACE-SAVING FRUIT TREES

Espalier, fan- and cordon-trained fruit trees need secure support from tiers of strong, galvanized wires. Fan-trained trees are best planted against a warm wall, while espaliers and cordons are ideal for growing as wall-trained trees and alongside paths, where they can be used to separate different parts of a garden.

Espalier

↗ Lateral branches on two sides are trained in equally spaced tiers. Ideal for apples and pears.

Fan-shaped

↗ Distinctive and ideal for planting against a wall. Not widely used for apples and pears; better for peaches and nectarines.

Cordons

↗ Single-stemmed trees growing at an angle of 45°. Ideal for apples and pears.

GROWING FOOD IN CONTAINERS

Vegetables on patios

Growing-bags are ideal for a wide range of vegetables (see details opposite for bush French beans, courgettes, lettuces and tomatoes). Additionally, cordon tomatoes can be grown in pots and placed against a warm wall. Grow bush tomatoes in a hanging-basket.

Apple trees in pots and tubs

There are three essential factors.

- Select wooden tubs or large terracotta pots, at least 38 cm (15 in) wide.
- Use dwarfing rootstocks, such as M27 or M9. Without their use, growing apples in containers is not practical.
- Buy a two-year-old tree, stake it firmly and train as a pyramid.

COST-EFFECTIVENESS

The cost of growing your own food on a small scale is higher than buying locally, but nothing can compare with harvesting your own home-grown food.

Herbs in containers

Many herbs are small and ideal for growing in containers on a patio, balcony or just in a windowbox.

- **Herb planters:** these resemble large pots, but with cupped, planting holes around their sides into which herbs can be put. Also, put herbs in the planter's top.
- **Growing-bags:** these are superb for mints (wide range).
- **Pots:** groups of herbs in individual pots look fine. They include chives, mint, parsley and thyme.
- **Windowboxes:** leave plants in their individual pots and pack moist peat around them.

Summer-flowering annuals

What is summer bedding?

Summer bedding is mainly formed of half-hardy annuals; they are raised from seeds sown each year in gentle warmth and, after acclimatization to outdoor conditions, planted into borders and beds when all risk of frost has passed. Occasionally, other plants are positioned among them to create focal points and variations in height (see page 23 for details of dot plants). Hardy annuals are grown in beds on their own, or as border fillers.

HARDY OR HALF-HARDY ANNUALS?

Both create colour during summer, but need slightly different treatment during their early stages.

- **Hardy annuals:** in spring they are sown outdoors in their growing positions. Sow them in shallow drills and when seedlings are large enough to handle remove some of them (called thinning) so that remaining ones have more space in which to grow and flower.
- **Half-hardy annuals:** more complex than hardy annuals and raised in gentle warmth in a greenhouse or on a shaded windowsill in late winter or early spring. Seedlings are transferred to wider spacings in other seed-trays, acclimatized (hardened off) to outdoor conditions and planted into borders when all risk of frost has passed. Because half-hardy annuals need more attention when being raised, they are more expensive than hardy annuals.

CLASSIC BEDDING COMBINATIONS

- **Border edging:** for a white-and-blue edging, alternate plants of *Lobularia maritima* (Sweet Alyssum) with those of *Lobelia erinus* (Edging Lobelia). Put two plants of Edging Lobelia between each Sweet Alyssum, because the latter are more vigorous.

- **Green edging:** plant a continuous line of *Tanacetum parthenium* 'Aureum' (see page 23) around a small bed and totally infill the area with red-flowered *Begonia semperflorens* (Wax Begonia) or blue-flowered *Ageratum*.

- **Pelargoniums:** often erroneously known as Geraniums, these are frequently included in formal bedding designs. Their range of colours is wide, with flowering throughout much of summer.

Agrostemma githago 'Milax'
Corn Cockle (UK/USA)

Purple Cockle (USA)

Hardy annual with light green leaves and masses of delicately veined, lilac-pink flowers from mid-summer to autumn.

Soil and situation: Grows in poor, moisture-retentive soil in full sun.

Raising new plants: From mid- to late spring sow seeds where they are to grow and flower. Sow in drills 6 mm (¼ in) deep and 25 cm (10 in) apart. Thin seedlings to 15–20 cm (6–8 in) apart.

↕ 90 cm–1 m (3–3½ ft) ↔ 38–45 cm (15–18 in)

Amaranthus caudatus 'Viridis'
Love-lies-bleeding (UK/USA)

Tassel Flower (USA)

Hardy annual with drooping tassels of pale, lime-green flowers from mid-summer to autumn.

Soil and situation: fertile, moisture-retentive but well-drained soil in full sun.

Raising new plants: from mid- to late spring sow seeds in flowering positions. Sow in drills 3 mm (⅛ in) deep and 25 cm (10 in) apart. Thin seedlings to 30 cm (12 in) apart.

↕ 90 cm–1 m (3–3½ ft) ↔ 38–45 cm (15–18 in)

Eschscholzia californica
Californian Poppy (UK/USA)

Hardy annual with blue-green leaves and masses of bright orange-yellow flowers from early to late summer. Colour range now includes scarlet, crimson, rose, orange, yellow, white and red.

Soil and situation: light, poor, well-drained soil in full sun.

Raising new plants: from early to late spring sow seeds where they are to grow and flower. Sow in drills 6 mm (¼ in) deep and 23 cm (9 in) apart. When large enough to handle, thin seedlings to 15–23 cm (6–9 in) apart.

↕ 30–38 cm (12–15 in) ↔ 15–23 cm (6–9 in)

Limnanthes douglasii

Meadow Foam (USA)

Poached Egg Flower (UK)

Hardy annual with masses of fragrant, funnel-shaped, yellow flowers with white edges from early to late summer.

Soil and situation: light, well-drained soil in full sun.

Raising new plants: from early to late spring sow seeds where they are to grow and flower. Sow in drills 3 mm (⅛ in) deep and 15 cm (6 in) apart. Thin seedlings to 15 cm (6 in) apart.

↕ 15 cm (6 in) ↔ 15–23 cm (6–9 in)

Lobularia maritima

Sweet Alyssum (UK/USA)

Also known as *Alyssum maritimum*, this hardy annual is usually grown as a half-hardy annual. Clusters of white, violet-purple or rose-carmine flowers from early to late summer.

Soil and situation: moderately fertile, well-drained soil in full sun.

Raising new plants: during late winter and early spring sow seeds shallowly in seed-trays in 10–13°C (50–55°F). Transfer seedlings to wider spacings in other seed-trays, reduce temperature and plant in a border when all risk of frost has passed.

↕ 7.5–15 cm (3–6 in) ↔ 20–25 cm (8–10 in)

Petunia x hybrida

Half-hardy perennial usually grown as a half-hardy annual. Trumpet-shaped flowers throughout summer, in colours including white, cream, pink, red, mauve and blue.

Soil and situation: fertile, well-drained but moisture-retentive soil in full sun.

Raising new plants: from late winter to early spring, sow seeds on surface of compost in 15–18°C (59–64°F). Transfer seedlings to wider spacings in other seed-trays, reduce temperature and plant in a border when all risk of frost has passed.

↕ 15–30 cm (6–12 in) ↔ 15–30 cm (6–12 in)

OTHER SUMMER-FLOWERING ANNUALS

- *Antirrhinum majus* (**Snapdragon**): usually grown as a half-hardy annual, as well as a hardy annual and even a hardy perennial. Masses of irregularly shaped flowers in a wide colour range.
- *Begonia semperflorens* (**Fibrous-rooted Begonia/Wax Begonia**): tender perennial usually grown as a half-hardy annual. Glossy, bright green or purple leaves surmounted by red, pink or white flowers.
- *Chrysanthemum carinatum* (**Annual Chrysanthemum/ Tricolored Chrysanthemum**): also known as *Chrysanthemum tricolor*, this hardy annual has large, daisy-like flowers with contrasting colour bandings.
- *Cleome spinosa* (**Spider Flower**): half-hardy annual with an erect habit and pink-flushed white flowers. Other colours include pink, rose, lilac, purple and white.
- *Heliotropium arborescens* (**Cherry Pie/Heliotrope**): half-hardy perennial, invariably grown as a half-hardy annual. Fragrant, forget-me-not-like flowers, in colours ranging from dark violet, through lavender, to white.
- *Lavatera trimestris* (**Annual Mallow**): bushy, hardy annual with trumpet-shaped, rose-coloured flowers.
- *Linum grandiflorum* 'Rubrum' (**Scarlet Flax**): hardy annual with brilliant crimson flowers.
- *Gypsophila elegans* (**Baby's Breath**): hardy annual with masses of white flowers. Several superb varieties, extending the colours to pink, rose-pink, carmine and soft purple.

- *Nicotiana alata* (**Flowering Tobacco Plant**): half-hardy annual with erect stems bearing loose clusters of richly scented, white, tubular flowers. Varieties in colours such as white, cream, pink, crimson, yellow and yellowish-green.
- *Lobelia erinus* (**Edging Lobelia/Trailing Lobelia**): half-hardy perennial invariably grown as a half-hardy annual, with masses of blue, white or red flowers. Some varieties are bushy, others trailing.
- *Malcolmia maritima* (**Virginian Stock**): hardy annual with sweetly scented, cross-shaped flowers in white, pink, red, lavender and purple.
- *Matthiola bicornis* (**Night-scented Stock**): hardy annual with masses of four-petalled, scented, lilac-purple flowers.
- *Nigella damascena* (**Love-in-a-Mist**): hardy annual with fern-like foliage and blue or white flowers.
- *Papaver rhoeas* (**Field Poppy**): hardy annual with 7.5 cm (3 in), red flowers with black centres. Varieties extend the colour range of pink, rose, salmon and crimson.
- *Salvia splendens* (**Scarlet Salvia**): half-hardy perennial invariably grown as a half-hardy annual. Scarlet flowers.
- *Tagetes erecta* (**African Marigold**): half-hardy annual with deeply divided leaves and lemon-yellow flowers. Range of varieties, some dwarf.
- *Tagetes patula* (**French Marigold**): half-hardy annual with yellow or mahogany-red flowers from early summer to autumn. Wide range of varieties – single and double-flowers, and dwarf forms.

Spring-flowering bedding plants

Are these mainly biennials?

The majority of spring-flowering bedding plants are biennials, which have a two-year growing cycle (see below). Several biennials are ideal companions for bulbous plants, such as Tulips, and some attractive combinations of them are suggested below. Additionally, some biennials – *Digitalis purpurea* (Foxgloves) and *Alcea rosea* (Hollyhocks) – have an informal character that makes them perfect for planting in a cottage garden or informal border.

NATURE OF BIENNIALS

Biennials are raised from seeds sown during one year for flowering in the following one. However, not everything with biennials is straightforward and although some, such as Foxgloves and Forget-me-nots, are natural biennials, others, like Hollyhocks, Daisies and Wallflowers, are hardy perennials usually grown as biennials.

During late spring and early summer sow seeds in a well-drained, outdoor seedbed in drills usually 6 mm (¼ in) deep (for specific depths for each biennial, see below). When large enough to handle, thin seedlings (see individual plant descriptions for spacings) to give plants more space in which to develop. In late summer or early autumn, move them to their flowering positions, spacing them as indicated on these pages. Some biennials, such as Hollyhocks with their cottage-garden nature, flower throughout much of summer.

CLASSIC SPRING COMBINATIONS

Tulips are popular for growing with biennials to create attractive shape and colour contrasts in spring. Here are a few to consider.

- Tulips are traditional companions for Wallflowers and Forget-me-nots. Cottage-type Tulips, with their large, egg-shaped heads, stand proudly above these underplantings.

- Tulips blend with a carpet planting of Double Daisies. For harmonies in blue, plant blue-flowered Parrot-type Tulips with Forget-me-nots.

- Choose dark red Darwin-type Tulips and combine them with white Pansies.

- Plant the single-early Tulip 'Keizerskroon' (with yellow and red flowers) with an underplanting of a yellow Viola.

Alcea rosea
Hollyhock (UK/USA)

Earlier known as *Althaea rosea*, this hardy perennial is usually grown as a biennial, and occasionally as an annual. From mid- to late summer it has tall stems with flowers in colours including yellow, pink, red and white. Some have double flowers.

Soil and situation: fertile, moisture-retentive soil in a sheltered position.

Raising new plants: in early and mid-summer, sow in drills 6 mm (¼ in) deep; thin seedlings to 25–30 cm (10–12 in) apart; plant 45–60 cm (1½–2 ft) apart.

↕ 1.5–1.8 m (5–6 ft) ↔ 45–60 cm (1½–2 ft)

Bellis perennis
Common Daisy (UK/USA)

Hardy perennial usually grown as a biennial, with bright-faced white flowers tinged pink and with a central yellow disc. There are several varieties, in colours including white, carmine, pink, salmon and rich cherry.

Soil and situation: fertile, well-drained but moisture-retentive soil in full sun or light shade.

Raising new plants: in late spring and early summer, sow seeds 6 mm (¼ in) deep; thin seedlings to 7.5 cm (3 in) apart; plant 13–15 cm (5–6 in) apart.

↕ 2.5–10 cm (1–4 in) ↔ 7.5–10 cm (3–4 in)

Campanula medium
Canterbury Bell (UK/USA)

Hardy biennial with upright stems bearing white, pink, blue or violet bell-shaped flowers from late spring to mid-summer.

Soil and situation: moderately fertile, well-drained soil in full sun.

Raising new plants: from mid-spring to early summer, sow seeds 6 mm (¼ in) deep; thin seedlings to 23 cm (9 in) apart; plant 25–30 cm (10–12 in) apart.

↕ 38–90 cm (15–90 cm) ↔ 23–30 cm (9–12 in)

Dianthus barbatus
Sweet William (UK/USA)

Short-lived perennial, invariably grown as a biennial, with large, flattened heads packed with sweetly scented, single or double flowers during early and mid-summer. Wide colour range, including crimson, scarlet, salmon-pink and cerise-pink.

Soil and situation: well-drained soil in full sun.

Raising new plants: in late spring and early summer, sow seeds 6 mm (¼ in) deep; thin seedlings to 13–15 cm (5–6 in) apart; plant 25–30 cm (10–12 in) apart.

↕ 30–60 cm (12–24 in)   ↔ 20–38 cm (8–15 in)

Digitalis purpurea
Common Foxglove (UK/USA)

Hardy biennial with an informal nature and stiff, upright stems bearing a profusion of bell-shaped flowers during early and mid-summer. They range in colour from purple, through pink, to red.

Soil and situation: grows well in moisture-retentive soil in light shade.

Raising new plants: in late spring and early summer, scatter seeds on surface of an outdoor seedbed and lightly rake in; thin seedlings to 15 cm (6 in) apart; plant 38–45 cm (13–18 in) apart.

↕ 90 cm–1.5 m (3–5 ft)   ↔ 45 cm (18 in)

Erysimum x allionii
Siberian Wallflower (UK)

Also known as *Cheiranthus x allionii*, this hardy, bushy perennial is invariably grown as a biennial. It develops scented, orange flowers in terminal clusters from mid-spring to early summer.

Soil and situation: fertile, well-drained, slightly chalky soil in full sun.

Raising new plants: in late spring and early summer, sow seeds 6 mm (¼ in) deep; thin seedlings to 13–15 cm (5–6 in) apart; plant 25–30 cm (10–12 in) apart. Pinch out the growing tips of young plants to encourage bushiness.

↕ 0–38 cm (12–15 in)   ↔ 25–30 cm (10–12 in)

Myosotis sylvatica
Forget-me-not (UK/USA)

Garden Forget-me-not (USA)

Hardy biennial or short-lived perennial with masses of fragrant, misty-blue flowers in late spring and early summer.

Soil and situation: fertile, moisture-retentive soil in partial shade.

Raising new plants: from late spring to mid-summer, sow seeds 6 mm (¼ in) deep; thin seedlings to 10–15 cm (4–6 in) apart; plant 15 cm (6 in) apart.

↕ 20–30 cm (8–12 in)   ↔ 15–20 cm (6–8 in)

OTHER SPRING-FLOWERING BEDDING PLANTS

The range of biennials that can be used in spring displays is wide, and apart from those that are illustrated on these pages there are several other reliable and attractive plants to consider:

- *Erysimum cheiri* (**Wallflower**): also known as *Cheiranthus cheiri*, this hardy perennial is invariably grown as a biennial. It displays sweetly scented flowers in terminal clusters from mid-spring to early summer. Flower colours include shades of red, yellow, orange, white and rose-pink. During late spring and early summer, sow seeds 6 mm (¼ in) deep; thin seedlings to 15 cm (6 in) apart; plant 25–38 cm (10–15 in) apart.

- *Erysimum hieraciifolium* (**Alpine Wallflower/Fairy Wallflower**): also known as *Erysimum alpinum*, this hardy biennial produces mauve and pale yellow flowers during late spring. In late spring and early summer, sow seeds 6 mm (¼ in) deep; thin seedlings to 10 cm (4 in) apart; plant 10–15 cm (4–6 in) apart.

- *Hesperis matronalis* (**Sweet Rocket**): hardy but short-lived perennial sometimes grown as a biennial. It has an upright but lax habit and fragrant, white, mauve or purple flowers during early summer. From mid-spring to early summer, sow seeds 6 mm (¼ in) deep; thin seedlings to 15–20 cm (6–8 in) apart; plant 38–45 cm (15–18 in) apart.

- *Lunaria annua* (**Honesty/Silver Dollar**): hardy biennial with fragrant, purple flowers from late spring to early summer, followed by attractive seed-pods. During late spring and early summer, sow seeds 6–12 mm (¼–½ in) deep; thin seedlings to 15 cm (6 in) apart; plant 30 cm (12 in) apart.

- *Viola x wittrockiana* (**Garden Pansy**): hardy biennial, well known for flowers up to 7.5 cm (3 in) wide, in colours including red, blue, white and violet from late spring to mid-summer. During early and mid-summer, sow seeds 6 mm (¼ in) deep; thin seedlings to 10 cm (4 in) apart; plant 23 cm (9 in) apart. There are also summer- and winter-flowering types.

Herbaceous perennials

What are herbaceous perennials?

These perennial plants live for several years – usually three or four – before the congested clumps need to be lifted and divided. Young pieces from around the outside are replanted, while old, inner parts discarded. Each spring, plants develop fresh shoots which, in autumn, die down to ground level. Often, bulbous plants are grown in the same border, and these are collectively known as border plants. Together, they create magnificent displays.

IN SMALL GARDENS

When planning a herbaceous border in a small garden, it is quite probable that, rather than being wide and straight, the border will have to be small and perhaps in a corner. Alternatively, it is possible to create a small 'island bed' (cut out of a lawn and surrounded by grass) which can be viewed and admired from all sides. An island bed – no more than 2.1 m (7 ft) wide – is usually planted with herbaceous perennials that do not need staking. In a small garden this helps to avoid the need to store plant supports during winter.

Whether planting a corner or island bed – or even a narrow border alongside a lawn – do not just use low-growing plants. A variation in height creates a more interesting feature than one that is uniformly level. There are a great many tall and distinctive plants to consider, including *Agapanthus* (see below).

ATTRACTIVE COMBINATIONS

- **Yellow and blue:** plant *Alchemilla mollis* (Lady's Mantle), with light green leaves and sulphur-yellow flowers, in front of *Tradescantia* x *andersoniana* 'Isis' (Trinity Flower) with rich, royal purple flowers.

- **Silver, blue and yellow:** plant a blue-flowered *Agapanthus* (African Lily) next to *Achillea filipendulina* (Fern-leaf Yarrow), with lemon-yellow flowers, and surrounded by the silver-leaved *Stachys byzantina* (Lamb's Tongue or Lamb's Ear).

- **Yellow and variegated grasses:** for a dominant back-of-border display, plant *Achillea filipendulina* (Fern-leaf Yarrow) in front of the tall, white-and-green variegated perennial grass *Phalaris arundinacea* var. *picta*.

Achillea filipendulina
Fern-leaf Yarrow (UK/USA)

Hardy, herbaceous perennial with plate-like heads up to 15 cm (6 in) wide packed with lemon-yellow flowers from mid-summer to autumn. Cultivars include 'Cloth of Gold' (gold) and 'Gold Plate' (deep yellow). *Achillea* 'Coronation Gold' is deep yellow.

Soil and situation: fertile, well-drained but moisture-retentive soil in full sun.

Increasing plants: lift and divide congested plants in early spring; replant young pieces from around the outside.

↕ 90 cm–1.2 m (3–4 ft)   ↔ 75–90 cm (2½–3 ft)

Agapanthus praecox
African Lily (UK/USA)
Lily of the Nile (USA)

Half-hardy evergreen perennial with fleshy roots and large, umbrella-like heads of bright to pale blue flowers from mid- to late summer. There are many other superb *Agapanthus*.

Soil and situation: fertile, well-drained soil in full sun, sheltered from cold winds.

Increasing plants: lift and divide congested clumps in spring; replant only young pieces from around the outside.

↕ 60–75 cm (2–2½ ft)   ↔ 45 cm (18 in)

Alchemilla mollis
Lady's Mantle (UK/USA)

Hardy, herbaceous perennial with rounded, light green leaves and masses of tiny, sulphur-yellow flowers in loose sprays from early to late summer.

Soil and situation: moderately fertile, moisture-retentive but well-drained soil in full sun or light shade.

Increasing plants: lift and divide congested plants in autumn or spring, replanting only young parts from around the outside. Additionally, it produces many seedlings.

↕ 30–45 cm (12–18 in)   ↔ 38–50 cm (15–20 in)

Allium moly

Golden Leek (UK)

Lily Leek (UK/USA)

Yellow Onion (UK)

Bulbous, with a herbaceous nature and bright yellow, star-shaped flowers in umbrella-like clusters during early and mid-summer. Several bulbs planted together form an attractive feature.

Soil and situation: light, well-drained soil in full sun.

Increasing plants: lift and divide congested clumps in autumn; take care that the bulbs do not become dry before being replanted.

⬆ 25–30 cm (10–12 in)   ↔ 20–25 cm (8–10 in)

Aster sediformis

Also known as *Aster acris*, this hardy, herbaceous perennial bears lavender-blue flowers with golden centres in dense clusters during late summer and into autumn. There are many other attractive herbaceous asters for planting in borders, some flowering well into autumn.

Soil and situation: fertile, moisture-retentive but well-drained soil in full sun.

Increasing plants: lift and divide congested plants in spring, replanting young pieces from around the outside.

⬆ 60–75 cm (2–2½ ft)   ↔ 38–45 cm (15–18 in)

Astilbe x arendsii

Hardy, herbaceous perennial with fern-like leaves and feather-like, pyramidal heads of flowers from early to late summer. There are many varieties, in colours including pink, dark red, rose-red, lilac-rose and white.

Soil and situation: fertile, moisture-retentive soil in light shade or full sun.

Increasing plants: lift and divide congested plants in autumn or spring.

⬆ 60–75 cm (2–2½ ft)   ↔ 38–50 cm (15–20 in)

Camassia quamash

Camass (UK)

Quamash (UK/USA)

Bulbous-rooted perennial with clusters of star-shaped flowers in poker-like heads during early and mid-summer. The flower colour varies, from white to blue and purple.

Soil and situation: fertile, moisture-retentive soil in light shade or full sun.

Increasing plants: lift and divide congested clumps in autumn. Replant large bulbs immediately; place small ones in a nursery bed until large enough to be planted into a border.

⬆ 45–75 cm (1½–2½ ft)   ↔ 30–38 cm (13–15 in)

Coreopsis verticillata

Hardy, long-lived herbaceous perennial with finely divided leaves and masses of bright yellow flowers from early to late summer. Several varieties include 'Grandiflora' (rich yellow flowers) and 'Zagreb' (golden-yellow flowers on compact plants).

Soil and situation: well-drained but moisture-retentive soil in full sun.

Increasing plants: lift and divide congested plants in autumn or spring.

⬆ 45–60 cm (1½–2 ft)   ↔ 30–45 cm (1–1½ ft)

Erigeron speciosus

Fleabane (UK/USA)

Hardy, herbaceous perennial with masses of daisy-like, purple flowers from early to late summer. Many other superb Erigerons, including 'Charity' (light pink), 'Darkest of All' (deep violet-blue) and 'Dignity' (violet-blue).

Soil and situation: fertile, moisture-retentive yet well-drained soil in light shade or full sun.

Increasing plants: lift and divide congested plants in autumn or spring; replant young pieces from the outside.

⬆ 45–60 cm (1½–2 ft)   ↔ 30–38 cm (12–15 in)

Helenium autumnale
Sneezewort (UK/USA)

Hardy, herbaceous perennial with masses of daisy-like yellow flowers with large, central bosses from mid-summer to early autumn. There are several other superb Heleniums (many with heights ideal for small gardens) in colours including orange, copper, bronze-red and crimson-mahogany.

Soil and situation: well-drained but moisture-retentive soil in full sun.

Increasing plants: lift and divide congested plants in autumn or spring; replant young pieces from the outside.

⬆ 1.2 m (4 ft) ↔ 38–45 cm (15–18 in)

Hemerocallis thunbergii
Day Lily (UK/USA)

Hardy, herbaceous perennial with large, trumpet-shaped, sulphur-yellow flowers during early and mid-summer. There are many hybrids, in colours from golden-yellow to pink, orange and brick-red.

Soil and situation: fertile, moisture-retentive but well-drained soil in light shade or full sun.

Increasing plants: lift and divide congested plants in autumn or spring; replant young pieces from the outside.

⬆ 75–90 cm (2½–3 ft) ↔ 45–60 cm (1½–2 ft)

Kniphofia
Red Hot Poker (UK/USA)

Hardy, herbaceous perennials, with poker-like flowerheads from early summer to autumn. Range of hybrids is wide, from cream and yellow to fiery-red, and in many heights, from 60 cm (2 ft) to 1.5 m (5 ft).

Soil and situation: well-drained soil in full sun; avoid those that are wet in winter and excessively fertile.

Increasing plants: lift and divide congested plants in early spring; avoid unnecessary damage to the crowns.

⬆ 60 cm–1.5 m (2–5 ft) ↔ 38–60 cm (15–24 in)

Leucanthemum x superbum
Max Daisy (USA)

Shasta Daisy (UK)

Also known as *Chrysanthemum maximum*, this hardy, herbaceous perennial has large, white, daisy-like flowers with boss-like, golden centres from early to late summer. Several superb varieties.

Soil and situation: fertile, slightly alkaline, well-drained but moisture-retentive soil in full sun.

Increasing plants: lift and divide congested clumps in early spring; replant young pieces from around the outside.

⬆ 75–90 cm (2½–3 ft) ↔ 30–45 cm (1–1½ ft)

Lysimachia punctata
Dotted Loosestrife (UK)

Yellow Loosestrife (UK)

Long-lived and slightly invasive herbaceous perennial with bright yellow, cup-shaped flowers produced from early to late summer.

Soil and situation: moderately fertile, moisture-retentive but well-drained soil in partial shade or full sun.

Increasing plants: lift and divide congested plants in autumn or early spring. Replant young pieces from around the outside of the clump.

⬆ 60–75 cm (2–2½ ft) ↔ 38–45 cm (15–18 in)

Rudbeckia fulgida
Coneflower (UK/USA)

Hardy, herbaceous perennial with large, daisy-like flowers with yellow petals and large, purple-brown, cone-like centres from mid-summer to autumn. Several superb forms.

Soil and situation: well-drained but moisture-retentive soil in sun.

Increasing plants: lift and divide congested plants in autumn or spring, replanting young parts from around the outside of the clump.

⬆ 60–90 cm (2–3 ft) ↔ 45–60 cm (1½–2 ft)

Sedum 'Autumn Joy'

Also known as *Sedum* 'Herbstfreude', this hardy herbaceous perennial has fleshy leaves. During late summer it has large heads of salmon-pink flowers that slowly change through orange-red to orange-brown in mid- to late autumn.

Soil and situation: light, moisture-retentive but well-drained soil in full sun.

Increasing plants: lift and divide congested plants in mid-spring; replant young pieces from around the outside.

↕ 45 cm (1½ ft)   ↔ 45–50 cm (18–20 in)

Solidago Hybrids

Golden Rod (UK/USA)

Hardy, herbaceous perennials with plume-like flower clusters from mid-summer to autumn. There are many hybrids, some with a dwarf nature and others more dominant.

Soil and situation: moderately fertile, well-drained soil in light shade or sun.

Increasing plants: lift and divide congested plants in autumn or spring, replanting young pieces from around the outside of the clump.

↕ 90 cm–1.5 m (3–5 ft)   ↔ 25–60 cm (10–24 in)

Tradescantia x andersoniana 'Isis'

Spiderwort (UK/USA)

Trinity Flower (UK/USA)

Also known as *Tradescantia virginiana* 'Isis', this hardy herbaceous perennial bears rich, royal purple flowers from early to late summer. Other varieties include 'Osprey' (white) and 'Purple Dome' (rich purple).

Soil and situation: moderately fertile, well-drained but moisture-retentive soil in light shade or full sun.

Increasing plants: lift and divide congested plants in spring; replant young pieces from the outside of the clump.

↕ 45–60 cm (1½–2 ft)   ↔ 45–50 cm (18–20 in)

OTHER HERBACEOUS PLANTS

- *Acanthus spinosus* (**Artist's Acanthus/Bear's Breeches**): hardy, herbaceous perennial with deeply cut, spiny leaves and tall spires of white and purple flowers during mid- and late summer.
- *Anemone* x *hybrida* (**Japanese Anemone/Japanese Windflower**): hardy, herbaceous perennial with upright stems bearing white to deep rose flowers from late summer to autumn.
- *Aruncus dioicus* (**Goat's Beard**): hardy, herbaceous perennial with lax, terminal heads of creamy-white flowers during early summer.
- *Bergenia cordifolia*: distinctive, hardy, border plant with rounded, evergreen leaves and drooping clusters of pale-pink, bell-shaped flowers during early and mid-spring.
- *Delphinium elatum*: hardy, herbaceous perennial, with two distinct forms: Elatum types have stiffly erect spires, tightly packed with large florets in several colours; Belladonna types have a more lax and graceful nature.
- *Echinacea purpurea* (**Purple Cone Flower**): hardy, herbaceous perennial that produces large, purple-crimson flowers up to 10 cm (4 in) wide from mid-summer through to autumn. Each flower has a distinctive cone-shaped, orange centre.
- *Geranium endressii* (**Crane's-bill**): hardy, herbaceous perennial with a ground-smothering habit and deeply lobed leaves and pale-pink flowers from early summer right through to autumn.
- *Gypsophila paniculata* (**Baby's Breath**): hardy, herbaceous perennial with masses of small, white flowers from early to late summer.
- *Helleborus niger* (**Christmas Rose**): hardy, perennial with evergreen, dark green leaves. From mid-winter to early spring it bears white flowers with golden anthers.
- *Lupinus polyphyllus* (**Lupin**): hardy, herbaceous perennial with tall stems bearing blue or red flowers during early and mid-summer. Russell Lupins have flowers in white, red, carmine, yellow, pink or orange.
- *Lychnis chalcedonica* (**Jerusalem Cross/Maltese Cross**): hardy, herbaceous perennial with small, bright scarlet flowers in flattened heads during mid- and late summer.
- *Monarda didyma* (**Bee Balm/Oswego Tea**): hardy, herbaceous perennial with bright scarlet flowers from early to late summer. Varieties in pink, lavender, violet-purple and white.
- *Phlox paniculata* (**Fall Phlox/Summer Phlox**): hardy, herbaceous perennial with terminal clusters of purple flowers from mid-summer to autumn. There are several varieties, in other colours.
- *Stachys byzantina* (**Lamb's Ear/Lamb's Tongue**): half-hardy herbaceous perennial with leaves covered with silvery hairs. During mid-summer it bears purple flowers.
- *Trollius* x *cultorum* (**Globe Flower**): Hardy, moisture-loving herbaceous perennial with large, buttercup-like flowers during late spring and early summer.

Shrubs and small trees

Is there a wide choice for a small garden?

Many shrubs and trees are ideal for growing in small gardens; some have a ground-covering habit while others help to create height, but not excessively. Some shrubs are famed for their flowers, and others have attractive leaves or berries. Most of these shrubs are fully hardy and will survive winter weather in temperate areas. On these and the following two pages, a wide range of shrubs and small trees is described, with some illustrated.

QUALITIES TO LOOK FOR

- **Naturally small:** although diminutive, a shrub or tree should reveal a natural and attractive appearance and not have to be radically pruned in an attempt to keep it small – which invariably does not work.
- **Slow-growing:** avoid shrubs and trees that grow rapidly and soon become too big for their allotted positions. Excessively vigorous plants are a waste of money, as too soon they have to be dug up and removed.
- **Varying interest:** wherever possible, select a shrub or tree that has at least two attractive qualities.
- **Easy to establish:** rapid and easy establishment are essential, so always buy a healthy plant. Do not buy an inferior plant just because it is cheap.
- **Non-invasive:** check that the plant is not invasive – meaning that it could soon dominate nearby plants.

ATTRACTIVE COMBINATIONS

- Plant yellow-flowered, trumpet-type Daffodils around *Amelanchier lamarckii* (Snowy Mespilus), a deciduous shrub or small tree with pure white flowers in spring and coloured leaves in autumn.

- Plant groups of *Helleborus foetidus* (Stinking Hellebore), with yellow-green flowers in early spring, around *Chimonanthus praecox* (Winter Sweet), which produces sweetly scented yellow flowers during mid- and late winter – and sometimes later. For further colour, add a few *Galanthus nivalis* (Snowdrops) to the picture.

- Plant *Lavandula angustifolia* (Old English Lavender) around a bed of pale pink bush roses.

Amelanchier lamarckii
June Berry (UK/USA)

Snowy Mespilus (UK)

Hardy, deciduous shrub or small tree with pure white flowers in mid-spring. Colourful leaves in autumn – shades of soft yellow and red.

Soil and situation: lime-free, moisture-retentive but well-drained soil in light shade or full sun.

Increasing plants: layer low-growing stems in late summer or early autumn. Alternatively, detach sucker-like shoots in spring and plant into a nursery bed.

↕ 3–4.5 m (10–15 ft) ↔ 3–3.6 m (10–12 ft)

Brachyglottis 'Sunshine'
Also known as *Senecio* 'Sunshine', this mound-forming, evergreen shrub has silvery-grey leaves and daisy-like, bright yellow flowers during early and mid-summer.

Soil and situation: deeply prepared, well-drained but moisture-retentive soil in full sun.

Increasing plants: layer low-growing stems in late summer. Rooting takes about a year. Alternatively, take 7.5–10 cm (3–4 in) long cuttings in late summer and insert in pots of equal parts moist peat and sharp sand. Place in a cold frame.

↕ 60 cm–1.2 m (2–4 ft) ↔ 90 cm–1.5 m (3–5 ft)

Caryopteris x clandonensis
Bluebeard (UK/USA)

Bushy, deciduous shrub with grey-green leaves and clusters of blue flowers in late summer and autumn. Varieties include 'Arthur Simmonds' (bright blue) and 'Heavenly Blue' (deep blue).

Soil and situation: moderately fertile, well-drained soil in full sun and shelter from cold wind.

Increasing plants: take 7.5–10 cm (3–4 in) long cuttings in late summer and insert in pots of equal parts moist peat and sharp sand in a cold frame.

↕ 60 cm–1.2 m (2–4 ft) ↔ 60–90 cm (2–3 ft)

Ceratostigma willmottianum

Chinese Plumbago (USA)

Hardy Plumbago (UK)

Half-hardy, deciduous shrub with dark green leaves that assume rich-red shades in autumn. During mid- and late summer it has terminal clusters of blue flowers.

Soil and situation: fertile, well-drained but moisture-retentive soil in light shade or full sun.

Increasing plants: take 7.5–10 cm (3–4 in) long cuttings in mid-summer and insert in pots of equal parts moist peat and sharp sand in gentle warmth.

↕ 60–90 cm (2–3 ft) ↔ 60–90 cm (2–3 ft)

Choisya ternata

Mexican Orange Blossom (UK/USA)

Slightly tender evergreen shrub with a bushy nature and clusters of sweetly scented, orange-blossom-like white flowers mainly in mid- and late spring, and intermittently throughout summer.

Soil and situation: deeply prepared, fertile, well-drained soil in light shade or full sun.

Increasing plants: take 7.5 cm (3 in) long cuttings in mid-summer and insert in pots of equal parts moist peat and sharp sand in gentle warmth.

↕ 1.5–1.8 m (5–6 ft) ↔ 1.5–2.1 m (5–7 ft)

Cistus x dansereaui

Rock Rose (UK/USA)

Sun Rose (UK)

Also known as *Cistus x lusitanicus*, this evergreen shrub has white flowers, 5 cm (2 in) wide and splashed with crimson, during early and mid-summer.

Soil and situation: poor, light, well-drained soil in full sun and shelter from cold wind.

Increasing plants: take 7.5 cm (3 in) long cuttings in mid-summer. Insert them in pots of equal parts moist peat and sharp sand in gentle warmth.

↕ 30–60 cm (1–2 ft) ↔ 45–60 cm (1½–2 ft)

Euonymus fortunei 'Emerald 'n' Gold'

Hardy, dwarf, evergreen shrub with golden variegated leaves that in winter assume bronzy-pinks tones. Other forms include 'Emerald Gaiety' (creamy-white and green) and 'Harlequin' (spring leaves mottled white and green).

Soil and situation: moderately fertile garden soil in light shade or full sun (which gives the best leaf colours).

Increasing plants: layer low-growing stems in autumn. Rooting takes about a year.

↕ 30–45 cm (1–1½ ft) ↔ 45–60 cm (1½–2 ft)

Forsythia x intermedia

Golden Bells (UK/USA)

Hardy, deciduous shrub with masses of golden-yellow flowers in early and mid-spring. The leaves start to appear as flowering finishes.

Soil and situation: fertile, deeply prepared, moisture-retentive soil in light shade or full sun.

Increasing plants: take 25 cm (10 in) long cuttings of the current season's shoots in early autumn and insert 10–15 cm (4–6 in) deep in a nursery bed. Sprinkle sharp sand around each cutting's base.

↕ 1.8–2.4 m (6–8 ft) ↔ 1.5–2.1 m (5–7 ft)

Hebe 'Autumn Glory'

Shrubby Veronica (UK)

Hardy, evergreen shrub with glossy leaves and deep purplish-blue flowers from mid-summer to autumn. 'Midsummer Beauty' has lavender-purple flowers and grows to about 1.2 m (4 ft).

Soil and situation: moderately fertile, well-drained soil in full sun.

Increasing plants: take 7.5–10 cm (3–4 in) long cuttings from non-flowering shoots in mid-summer. Insert them in pots of equal parts moist peat and sharp sand in a cold frame.

↕ 60–75 cm (2–2½ ft) ↔ 60–75 cm (2–2½ ft)

Helichrysum italicum
Curry Plant (UK)

Also known as *Helichrysum angustifolium*, an evergreen shrub with narrow, silvery-grey, needle-like leaves that reveal the bouquet of curry. Mustard-yellow flowers throughout much of summer.

Soil and situation: light, moderately poor, well-drained soil in full sun. Avoid wet and cold soils.

Increasing plants: take 7.5 cm (3 in) long cuttings from the current season's shoots in mid-summer; insert in sandy compost and place in a cold frame.

↕ 30–38 cm (12–15 in)   ↔ 38–60 cm (15–24 in)

Hypericum 'Hidcote'
Rose of Sharon (UK/USA)

Hardy, almost evergreen, bushy shrub. From mid-summer to autumn it bears 7.5 cm (3 in) wide, saucer-shaped, waxy, golden-yellow flowers.

Soil and situation: fertile, moisture-retentive but well-drained soil and full sun. Avoid positions in shade.

Increasing plants: take 10–13 cm (4–5 in) long cuttings from the current season's shoots in mid-summer. Insert in pots of equal parts moist peat and sharp sand and place in a cold frame.

↕ 90 cm–1.5 m (3–5 ft)   ↔ 1.5–2.1 m (5–7 ft)

Magnolia stellata
Star Magnolia (UK/USA)

Hardy, slow-growing deciduous shrub with a rounded nature and fragrant, star-shaped flowers up to 10 cm (4 in) wide during early and mid-spring. Several forms, including 'Waterlily' with petal-packed flowers.

Soil and situation: deeply prepared, well-drained but moisture-retentive soil in full sun and a wind-sheltered position.

Increasing plants: layer low-growing branches in early summer. Rooting takes up to two years.

↕ 2.4–3 m (8–10 ft)   ↔ 2.4–3 m (8–10 ft)

Philadelphus Hybrids
Mock Orange (UK/USA)

Hardy, deciduous shrubs with single or double, sweetly scented, white, cup-shaped flowers during early and mid-summer. Many hybrids are ideal for small gardens. 'Avalanche' is 90 cm–1.5 m (3–5 ft) high.

Soil and situation: moderately fertile, well-drained yet moisture-retentive soil in partial shade or full sun.

Increasing plants: take 25–30 cm (10–12 in) long hardwood cuttings in autumn and insert 15 cm (6 in) deep in a nursery bed.

↕ 90 cm–3 m (3–10 ft)   ↔ 90 cm–3.6 m (3–12 ft)

Potentilla fruticosa
Shrubby Cinquefoil (UK/USA)

Hardy, deciduous, bushy but compact shrub with masses of buttercup-yellow flowers from early to late summer – and sometimes into autumn. Several hybrids, in colours including soft yellow, glowing-red and tangerine-red.

Soil and situation: light, moisture-retentive but well-drained soil in full sun.

Increasing plants: take 7.5 cm (3 in) long cuttings from the current season's shoots during late summer. Place in a cold frame.

↕ 1–1.2 m (3½–4 ft)   ↔ 1–1.2 m (3½–4 ft)

Salvia officinalis 'Icterina'

Slightly tender, short-lived, evergreen shrub (semi-evergreen in cold areas) with green-and-gold variegated leaves. Related forms include 'Purpurescens' (young leaves suffused purple) and 'Tricolor' (grey-green leaves splashed creamy-white).

Soil and situation: light, well-drained soil in full sun, sheltered from cold wind.

Increasing plants: take 7.5 cm (3 in) long cuttings in late summer and insert in equal parts moist peat and sharp sand. Place in a cold frame.

↕ 45–60 cm (1½–2 ft)   ↔ 38–45 cm (15–18 in)

Spiraea 'Arguta'
Bridal Wreath (UK)

Foam of May (UK)

Hardy, deciduous shrub with attractive mid-green leaves and masses of pure white flowers in mid- and late spring.

Soil and situation: fertile, deep-prepared, moisture-retentive but well-drained soil in full sun.

Increasing plants: take 7.5–10 cm (3–4 in) long cuttings from the current season's shoots in mid-summer. Insert in pots of equal parts moist peat and sharp sand and place in a cold frame.

↕ 1.8–2.4 m (6–8 ft) ↔ 1.5–1.8 m (5–6 ft)

Syringa meyeri
Hardy, deciduous, small-leaved lilac with violet-purple flowers borne in small, rounded clusters up to 10 cm (4 in) long during early summer. Occasionally, there is a further flush of flowers.

Soil and situation: fertile, deep prepared, well-drained but moisture-retentive soil in light shade or full sun.

Increasing plants: take 7.5 cm (3 in) long cuttings with heels during mid-summer and insert in pots of equal parts moist peat and sharp sand. Place in gentle warmth.

↕ 1.5–1.8 m (5–6 ft) ↔ 1.2–1.5 m (4–5 ft)

Weigela Hybrids
Hardy, deciduous shrubs with arching branches and masses of flowers during early summer. There are many superb varieties, including 'Abel Carrière' (bright red), 'Bristol Ruby' (ruby-red) and 'Newport Red' (bright red).

Soil and situation: fertile, deeply prepared, well-drained but moisture-retentive soil in light shade or full sun.

Increasing plants: take 25–30 cm (10–12 in) long cuttings from mature shoots of the current season's growth during autumn. Insert them about 15 cm (6 in) deep in a nursery bed.

↕ 1.5–1.8 m (5–6 ft) ↔ 1.5–2.4 m (5–8 ft)

OTHER SHRUBS AND TREES

- *Berberis darwinii* (**Darwin's Berberis**): hardy, evergreen shrub with deep yellow flowers in mid- and late spring. Small, prickly, holly-like leaves.
- *Buddleja davidii* (**Butterfly Bush/Orange-eye Buddleia/Summer Lilac**): also known as *Buddleia davidii*, this hardy, deciduous shrub is well known for its long, often arching stems that bear large, plume-like heads of fragrant, lilac-purple flowers during mid- and late summer. There are many varieties, in colours including dark violet, mauve, and white.
- *Calluna vulgaris* '**Gold Haze**' (**Heather/Ling/Scotch Heather**): hardy, evergreen, low, mound-forming shrub with golden-yellow foliage; white flowers during late summer and into early autumn.
- *Cytisus* × *kewensis*: sprawling, deciduous shrub with mid-green leaves and masses of pale yellow flowers during late spring and early summer.
- *Cytisus* × *praecox* (**Warminster Broom**): hardy, deciduous shrub with creamy-white flowers during late spring and early summer.
- *Daphne mezereum* (**February Daphne/Mezereon/Mezereum**): hardy, deciduous shrub with purple-red flowers from late winter to spring. These are borne on bare stems and followed by scarlet, poisonous berries.
- *Fuchsia magellanica* (**Hardy Fuchsia/Lady's Eardrops**): slightly tender shrub with crimson-and-purple flowers from mid-summer to autumn.
- *Hamamelis mollis* (**Chinese Witch Hazel**): hardy, deciduous shrub or small tree that produces sweetly scented, rich golden-yellow, spider-like flowers during early and mid-winter.
- *Hydrangea macrophylla* (**Common Hydrangea/French Hydrangea**): hardy, deciduous shrub; there are two forms – Hortensias with mop-like flowerheads and Lacecaps which have a more lax nature.
- *Kerria japonica* '**Pleniflora**' (**Bachelor's Buttons/Japanese Rose**): hardy, deciduous shrub with long, slender stems and double, orange-yellow flowers during late spring and early summer.
- *Mahonia* × *media* '**Charity**': hardy, evergreen shrub with distinctive, leathery leaves and long spires of fragrant, deep lemon-yellow flowers from early to late winter.
- *Paeonia suffruticosa* subsp. *rockii*: also known as 'Joseph Rock' and 'Rock's Variety', this slightly tender deciduous shrub bears white flowers, richly and prominently blotched in maroon-crimson, during early summer.
- *Philadelphus coronarius* '**Aureus**': hardy, deciduous shrub with a bushy nature and orange-blossom-scented, creamy-white flowers during early and mid-summer. However, it is best known for its beautiful golden-yellow foliage.
- *Romneya coulteri* var. *trichocalyx* (**Californian Tree Poppy/Tree Poppy**): hardy, semi-woody shrub with blue-green leaves and slightly fragrant, poppy-like, white flowers from mid- to late summer.

Wall shrubs

Why grow wall shrubs?

Ideal in a small garden, wall shrubs enable more plants to be grown in a space-restricted area. Additionally, tender shrubs need the warmth and wind protection of a sun-facing wall. Some wall shrubs are too vigorous for small gardens, but many have a manageable and adaptable nature that makes them ideal for constricted areas (see below). Their range is wide, from winter-flowering types to those that clothe walls in leaves, berries or flowers.

QUALITIES TO LOOK FOR

- **Manageable and adaptable:** a few wall shrubs can be restricted in size by training or pruning. For example, the deciduous *Cotoneaster horizontalis* (Fishbone Cotoneaster) spreads upwards and sideways along a wall; intrusive growth can be limited by pruning, but take care not to spoil the shrub's shape. *Jasminum nudiflorum* (Winter-flowering Jasmine) has pliable stems, and by tying these to wires its height can be limited – this is especially useful when growing it beneath a window.
- **Right aspect:** tender wall shrubs must be given a warm aspect, but *Jasminum nudiflorum* (Winter-flowering Jasmine) grows well against a sunless wall with a cold aspect.
- **Dwarf nature:** check that a wall shrub's height and spread will not overwhelm its position. Rapid removal means it has been an expensive buy.

OTHER WALL SHRUBS FOR SMALL GARDENS

- *Abutilon megapotamicum*: half-hardy, slender-stemmed, wall shrub with conspicuous flowers with yellow petals, red calyces and purple anthers throughout summer and into early autumn.
  Height: 1.5–2.1 m (5–7 ft) Spread: 1.5–2.1 m (5–7 ft)
- *Fremontodendron californicum*: also known as *Fremontia californica*, a slightly tender deciduous or semi-evergreen wall shrub with cup-shaped, golden-yellow flowers, up to 5 cm (2 in) wide, throughout summer and early autumn.
  Height: 1.8–3 m (6–10 ft) Spread: 1.8–3 m (6–10 ft)
- *Garrya elliptica* (**Silk Tassel Bush**): hardy, evergreen shrub with long, drooping, grey-green catkins in late winter – sometimes earlier in mild areas..
  Height: 2.4–3 m (8–10 ft) Spread: 1.8–3 m (6–10 ft)

Ceanothus thyrsiflorus var. repens
Blue Blossom (USA)

Californian Lilac (UK)

Evergreen, mound-forming shrub that can be trained against a wall. During late spring and early summer it bears small, light blue flowers in clusters.

Soil and situation: light, neutral to slightly acid, well-drained but moisture-retentive soil and a sheltered spot.

Increasing plants: take 7.5 cm (3 in) long cuttings in mid-summer and insert them in pots of equal parts moist peat and sharp sand. Place in gentle warmth.

↕ 1.2–1.5 m (4–5 ft) ↔ 1.2–1.8 m (4–6 ft)

Cotoneaster horizontalis
Fishbone Cotoneaster (UK)

Rock Cotoneaster (USA)

Hardy, low-growing and spreading deciduous shrub with branches initially horizontal but soon upright. Pink flowers appear in early summer, followed by red berries which persist well into winter.

Soil and situation: well-drained soil in full sun or partial shade.

Increasing plants: layer low-growing stems in late summer or autumn. Rooting takes up to two years.

↕ 60–90 cm (2–3 ft) ↔ 1.2–1.8 m (4–6 ft)

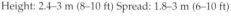

Jasminum nudiflorum
Winter-flowering Jasmine (UK)

Deciduous, lax, wall shrub with pliable stems. Bright yellow flowers are borne on bare, leafless stems from late autumn to late spring.

Soil and situation: well-drained soil and a position against a wall – it grows well against sunless, cold-facing walls.

Increasing plants: the easiest way is by layering low-growing stems in late summer or early autumn. Rooting takes about a year.

↕ 1.8–2.1 m (6–7 ft) ↔ 1.8–2.1 m (6–7 ft)

Climbers

The key to success with a climber in a small garden is not to choose a vigorous type. Forget about large, leafy climbers that create vast wall-coverings of coloured leaves in autumn. Instead, there are many flowering climbers, several with distinctively shaped flowers, that will delight you. For a leafy screen, choose the herbaceous climber *Humulus lupulus* 'Aureus' (Yellow-leaved Hop) – each spring it creates a fresh array of leaves.

Are climbers controllable?

CLIMBING HABITS

A climber's habit indicates the support it needs.
- **Leaners:** in the wild, they lean against a neighbour, but in a garden need a supporting framework. They include *Abutilon megapotamicum* and *Jasminum nudiflorum*.
- **Self-supporting:** these are successful climbers, using adhesive suckers and aerial roots to gain support. They include *Hedera helix* (Ivies).
- **Tendrils and twisting leaf-stalks:** in the wild, they need twiggy hosts, and in a garden a supporting framework. They include Clematis, *Lathyrus odoratus* (Sweet Pea) and *Passiflora caerulea* (Passion Flower).
- **Twiners:** these twine around their neighbours. In a garden they need support from a trellis or wires. They include *Humulus lupulus* 'Aureus' (Yellow-leaved Hop), *Lonicera* (Honeysuckles) and *Jasminum officinale* (White Jasmine).

OTHER CLEMATIS FOR SMALL GARDENS

- *Clematis alpina*: pretty, weak-growing but bushy, deciduous climber with pendulous, cup-shaped, violet-blue flowers during mid- and late spring. Several superb varieties, including 'Frances Rivis'.
  Height: 1.8–2.4 m (6–8 ft) Spread: 1.5–1.8 m (5–6 ft)
- *Clematis flammula*: hardy, deciduous, bushy climber with fragrant, pure white flowers during late summer and well into autumn. It is at its best when scrambling through other plants.
  Height: 2.4–3 m (8–10 ft) Spread: 1.5–1.8 m (5–6 ft)
- *Clematis macropetala*: slender, bushy, deciduous climber with light and dark blue, nodding, bell-shaped flowers during late spring and early summer.
  Height: 2.4–3.6 m (8–12 ft) Spread: 1.8–2.4 m (6–8 ft)

Clematis – Large-flowered Hybrids

Deciduous climbers with large flowers. Most are single-flowered, appearing during summer; the exact period depends on the variety. Wide colour range; some with a single colour, others with shading in bars or stripes.

Soil and situation: fertile, neutral to slightly alkaline soil and full sun – but with shade for the roots.

Increasing plants: take 7.5 cm (3 in) long cuttings from half-ripe shoots during mid-summer. Insert them in pots of equal parts moist-peat and sharp sand, and place in gentle warmth.

↕ 1.2–4.5 m (4–15 ft)   ↔ 1.2–3 m (4–10 ft)

Clematis chrysocoma

Hardy, deciduous climber, similar to *Clematis montana* (Mountain Clematis) but less vigorous. In early and mid-summer (sometimes later) it bears single, white, pink-tinged, saucer-shaped flowers.

Soil and situation: fertile, neutral to slightly alkaline soil in full sun – but with shade for the roots.

Increasing plants: take 7.5 cm (3 in) long cuttings from half-ripe shoots during mid-summer. Insert them in pots of equal parts moist peat and sharp sand and place in gentle warmth.

↕ 2.4–3m (8–10 ft)   ↔ 2.4–3m (8–10 ft)

Passiflora caerulea

Blue Passion Flower (USA)

Common Passion Flower (UK)

Slightly tender, scrambling, deciduous climber with spectacular flowers, about 7.5 cm (3 in) wide and with white petals and blue-purple centres, from early to late summer.

Soil and situation: moderately fertile, well-drained soil in light shade or sun.

Increasing plants: take 7.5 cm (3 in) long cuttings in mid-summer and insert in pots of equal parts moist peat and sharp sand. Place in gentle warmth.

↕ 1.8–3 m (6–10 ft)   ↔ 1.8–2.4 m (6–8 ft)

Rock-garden plants

What are rock-garden plants?

The range of plants grown in rock gardens is exceptionally wide, from true alpines to bulbs, dwarf conifers and shrubs. Yet the majority of plants are diminutive and colourful perennials, such as *Aurinia saxatilis* (also known as *Alyssum saxatile*), *Aubretia*, *Arabis* (Rock Cress) and Saxifrages. Incidentally, true alpine plants are found on mountains, below the permanent snow line and above the tree line. In a small rock garden, miniature plants are essential.

TYPES OF PLANTS

- **Bulbs and corms:** wide range of small types – see right for a selection. They have a dainty nature and many flower during winter or in spring.
- **Rock-garden perennials:** once planted, these create magnificent displays until they become congested and need to be lifted and divided. Many die down to ground level in autumn; new shoots appear in spring.
- **Annuals:** popular, inexpensive and ideal for filling bare areas in newly constructed rock gardens. Both hardy and half-hardy types are used.
- **Dwarf shrubs and trees:** deciduous and evergreen types, some prostrate, others upright or dome-shaped.
- **Miniature conifers:** distinctive and in several shapes, including conical, flattened, and bun-shaped. If they become too large, move them into a border.

MINIATURE BULBS TO CONSIDER

- *Chionodoxa luciliae* (**Glory of the Snow**): during late winter and early spring it creates a wealth of light blue, white-centred flowers.
- *Crocus chrysanthus*: golden-yellow, globe-shaped flowers are produced during late winter and early spring. Also, there are white, blue and purple forms.
- *Eranthis hyemalis* (**Winter Aconite**): bears lemon-yellow, cup-shaped flowers backed by a light-green ruff during late winter and spring.
- *Iris danfordiae*: honey-scented, vivid lemon flowers are produced during mid- and late winter.
- *Iris reticulata*: bluish-purple flowers with orange blazes appear during late winter and early spring.
- *Narcissus bulbocodium*: bears yellow, hoop-like flowers during late winter and early spring.

Aubrieta deltoidea

Hardy, low-growing, evergreen perennial with masses of cross-shaped flowers in shades of rose-lilac to purple from early spring to early summer.

Soil and situation: well-drained, preferably slightly chalky soil in full sun.

Increasing plants: sow seeds thinly and evenly in a seed-bed outdoors from mid-spring to early summer. Sow 6 mm (¼ in) deep in drill 20 cm (8 in) apart. Alternatively, divide congested plants in late summer or early autumn.

↕ 7.5–10 cm (3–4 in) ↔ 45–60 cm (1½–2 ft)

Aurinia saxatilis

Gold Dust (UK)

Also known as *Alyssum saxatile*, this hardy, shrubby evergreen has grey-green leaves and masses of clustered, yellow flowers from mid-spring to early summer. Varieties include 'Citrina' (bright lemon-gold) and 'Compacta' (dwarf and golden-yellow).

Soil and situation: well-drained soil and full sun.

Increasing plants: sow seeds in pots during early spring and place in a cold frame. Alternatively, take 5 cm (2 in) long cuttings in early summer.

↕ 20–25 cm (8–10 in) ↔ 30–45 cm (1–1½ ft)

Saxifraga cotyledon

Rosettes of dark green leaves and pure white, starry flowers borne in plume-like sprays from early to mid-summer. The form 'Southside Seedling' is ideal for planting in crevices between rocks.

Soil and situation: well-drained, gritty, slightly alkaline soil in a semi-shaded and sheltered position.

Increasing plants: detach non-flowering rosettes in early summer and insert in pots of equal parts moist peat and sharp sand. Place in a cold frame.

↕ 30–45 cm (1–1½ ft) ↔ 30–38 cm (12–15 in)

Water and marginal plants

Most ponds are made from a pre-formed shell or a flexible liner. Both have merits, and their durability depends on materials and construction. Don't rush construction – ensure pre-formed shells have a firm base and are not twisted, and that sharp objects cannot puncture flexible liners. The water's surface can be at ground level, or raised to make plants and fish easier to see. There is a wide range of plants for growing in and around a pond.

Is a pond easy to create?

TYPES OF PLANT

- **Bog-garden plants:** roots in constantly moist soil, with leaves, stems and flowers above the compost's surface. Also known as moisture-loving plants and waterside plants.
- **Deep-water aquatics:** submerged roots, with leaves and flowers on or above the water's surface.
- **Floaters:** leaves and stems float freely on the water's surface, with roots below and usually trailing.
- **Marginal plants:** roots submerged, with leaves and flowers above the water's surface. Positioned around the edge of a pond, but in the water.
- **Oxygenators:** all of the plant is submerged, with roots in a container. Also known as water weeds.
- **Waterlilies:** distinctive and popular, with roots submerged and leaves and flowers on the surface. Range of varieties and suitable for ponds of all sizes and depths.

WATERLILIES FOR ALL PONDS

There are varieties for many depths of water – measured from the rim of the container to the surface.
- **Pygmy Waterlilies:** water's depth – no more than 23 cm (9 in). Spread: 30–60 cm (1–2 ft).
- **Small Waterlilies:** water's depth – 15–45 cm (6–18 in). Spread: 60 cm–1.2 m (2–4 ft).
- **Medium Waterlilies:** water's depth – 30–60 cm (1–2 ft). Spread: 1.2–1.5 m (4–5 ft).
- **Vigorous Waterlilies:** water's depth – 45–90 cm (1½–3 ft). Spread: 1.5–2.4 m (5–8 ft).

PLANTING WATERLILIES

Buy Waterlilies in late spring or early summer, just when they are starting to grow. If there is a delay in planting, remember to keep the roots moist.

Iris pseudacorus 'Variegata'
Variegated Water Flag (USA)

Variegated Yellow Flag Iris (UK)

Marginal plant, with a herbaceous nature and erect, sword-like, bluish-green leaves with yellow stripes. It bears yellow flowers during early summer.

Soil and situation: fertile soil in water 15 cm (6 in) deep and in full sun.

Increasing plants: lift and divide congested clumps immediately after the flowers fade. Alternatively, divide when plants are growing actively and positions of the rhizomatous roots can be seen.

↕ 75–90 cm (2½–3 ft)   ↔ 38–45 cm (15–18 in)

Lysichiton americanus
Skunk Cabbage (UK/USA)

Western Skunk Cabbage (USA)

Yellow Skunk Cabbage (USA)

Bog-garden plant, with a hardy, herbaceous nature and oval, grass-green leaves up to 90 cm (3 ft) long. From early to late spring it produces flowers formed of deep, yellow spathes.

Soil and situation: fertile, moisture-retentive soil beside a garden pond.

Increasing plants: remove young plants from around the outside of a congested clump and plant in a pot – keep the compost moist.

↕ 60–90 cm (2–3 ft)   ↔ 60–75 cm (2–2½ ft)

Nymphaea species
Waterlily (UK/USA)

Many hardy Waterlilies for outdoor ponds. Perennial nature, with stems and leaves that die in autumn. Flowers appear in succession throughout summer, in colours including white, pink, red, copper and yellow.

Soil and situation: fertile, loamy soil in plastic-mesh containers. Pick varieties to suit the water's depth (see above).

Increasing plants: divide congested plants in early to mid-spring, when the pond is drained.

↕ water's surface   ↔ depends on vigour

Bamboos

What are bamboos?

Bamboos belong to the grass family. They are evergreen, with stiff, hollow stems that give them support. They usually form clumps and, while some are invasive and unsuitable for small gardens, others are non-invasive or can be easily controlled (see below). Once established, bamboos need little attention, other than ensuring they are not spreading too far. Some can be grown in containers and three of them are suggested below, but there are many others.

BAMBOOS IN CONTAINERS

The range of suitable bamboos is wide, with displays in several heights. In exceptionally windy areas, choose low-growing bamboos. Alternatively, give them a sheltered position next to a wind-filtering hedge.

Low display: 90 cm–1.2 m (3–4 ft)
• *Pleioblastus viridistriatus* (Golden-haired Bamboo): purple-green stems and brilliant golden-yellow variegated leaves with pea-green stripes.

Medium-height display: 1.8–2.4 m (6–8 ft)
• *Fargesia murieliae* (Umbrella Bamboo): bright green canes that mature to dull yellow, and dark green leaves.

Tall and dominant display: 2.4–3.6 m (8–12 ft)
• *Pseudosasa japonica* (Arrow Bamboo): canes olive-green at first, maturing to dull matt-green. Dark, glossy-green, sharply pointed leaves.

ARE BAMBOOS TOO INVASIVE FOR A SMALL GARDEN?

Some bamboos are very invasive and in a small garden may trespass into neighbouring properties. Bamboos can be classified according to their vigour.

• **Clump-forming and non-invasive:** these will not cause a problem and are ideal for small gardens. They include *Fargesia murieliae* (also known as *Arundinaria murieliae*) and *Fargesia nitida* (also known as *Arundinaria nitida*).

• **Moderately invasive but easily checked:** once established, regularly chopping back of young shoots will be necessary. Alternatively, install a proprietary metal barrier 15 cm (6 in) from the boundary and let into a trench 50 cm (20 in) deep. Position 7.5 cm (3 in) of the barrier above the surface.

• **Invasive:** these are rampant and therefore are not at all suitable for small gardens.

Fargesia murieliae
Umbrella Bamboo (UK/USA)

Also known as *Arundinaria murieliae*, this hardy, elegant, clump-forming and non-invasive bamboo has arching, bright green canes that mature to dull yellow. Narrow, oblong, dark green leaves.

Soil and situation: fertile, moisture-retentive but well-drained soil in light shade or full sun.

Increasing plants: lift and divide congested large clumps in spring, just as new growth is beginning.

↕ 1.8–2.4 m (6–8 ft)

Phyllostachys nigra
Black-stemmed Bamboo (UK/USA)
Black Bamboo (UK/USA)

Hardy, graceful, evergreen, clump-forming bamboo with canes first green but jet-black within 2–3 years. The leaves are dark green. It is moderately invasive but easily checked.

Soil and situation: fertile, moisture-retentive but well-drained soil in full sun. The stems achieve their best colour when in dry soil.

Increasing plants: lift and divide congested large clumps in spring, just as new growth is beginning.

↕ 2.4–3 m (8–10 ft)

Sasa veitchii
Kuma Bamboo Grass (USA)

Also known as *Arundinaria veitchii*, this hardy, invasive and low-growing bamboo has slender, purple-green canes. The glossy, smooth-surfaced, deep rich-green leaves are up to 25 cm (10 in) long. The canes are slender and purple-green.

Soil and situation: fertile, moisture-retentive but well-drained soil in dappled light.

Increasing plants: lift and divide congested large clumps in spring, just as new growth is beginning.

↕ 90 cm–1.5 m (3–5 ft)

Ornamental grasses

Unlike lawn grasses, ornamental types are ideal for planting or sowing in borders and beds in gardens. Some are annual, others herbaceous and few perennial; several uses of them are suggested below. Additionally, some grasses when dried are ideal for using in floral displays indoors. In the garden they are frequently used to introduce an artistic element, with unusual and distinctive shapes and colours that harmonize with other plants.

What are ornamental grasses?

HOW CAN I USE ORNAMENTAL GRASSES?

These grasses can be used in many ways in gardens.

- **Annual grasses:** filling bare areas in newly planted herbaceous or mixed borders. Within a few months of being sown, they create magnificent displays.
- **Herbaceous grasses:** in beds totally devoted to them, or mixed with medleys of other plants.
- **Perennial grasses:** these include grasses such as *Cortaderia selloana* (Pampas Grass), with long, fluffy flowerheads, which look good in a bed cut into a lawn.
- **Grasses in containers:** display on a patio (see right for a range of suitable plants).
- **Dominant grasses:** the majestic *Miscanthus sacchariflorus*, which grows up to 3 m (10 ft) high, can be used to create an attractive, unusual and practical screen.

GRASSES AND SEDGES IN CONTAINERS

Many grasses and sedges thrive in containers, but ensure that their roots do not become dry during summer. Sedges are especially damaged by dry soil.

- *Acorus gramineus* 'Ogon': initially upright, then arching, with narrow and tapering green leaves with golden variegated bands along their lengths.
- *Carex oshimensis* 'Evergold': arching nature, with leaves variegated green and yellow. There are several other *Carex* species that are suitable for containers.
- *Festuca glauca*: tufted nature, with coloured leaves and including blue, blue-green and silvery-blue. Ideal for containers with ornate sides that need to be admired.
- *Hakonechloa macra* 'Alboaurea': cascading nature, with long, arching, narrow leaves striped gold and off-white.

Coix lacryma-jobi
Christ's Tears (UK)

Job's Tears (UK/USA)

Half-hardy annual grass with broad, lance-shaped, pale to mid-green leaves. From mid-summer to early autumn it bears grey-green, woody, edible seeds that hang in tear-like clusters.

Soil and situation: fertile, moisture-retentive but well-drained soil in full sun.

Increasing plants: during late winter and early spring sow seeds shallowly in pots in gentle warmth. Plant into a border when all risk of frost has passed.

↕ 45–60 cm (1½–2 ft)   ↔ 25–30 cm (10–12 in)

Cortaderia selloana
Pampas Grass (UK/USA)

Perennial, evergreen grass with slender leaves and tall, woody stems that bear fluffy, silvery plumes up to 45 cm (18 in) long from late summer to late winter. For a small garden, it is best to plant the form 'Pumila'.

Soil and situation: fertile, moisture-retentive soil in full sun.

Increasing plants: lift and divide large clumps in spring, replanting young parts from around the outside. However, this usually results in spoiling the mother plant's shape.

↕ 1.5–2.4 m (5–8 ft)   ↔ 1.5–2.1 m (5–7 ft)

Hakonechloa macra 'Alboaurea'

Hardy, cascading, perennial grass with narrow, brightly variegated leaves. It is ideal for planting at the edge of a raised bed or in a pot on a patio. There are other attractive forms, including 'Aureola' (yellow leaves striped with narrow green lines).

Soil and situation: moderately fertile, well-drained soil in full sun.

Increasing plants: lift and divide congested plants in spring.

↕ 25–30 cm (10–12 in)   ↔ 75–90 cm (2½–3 ft)

Plants for containers

Which containers are best?

Where possible in a small garden, use containers such as windowboxes, wall-baskets, mangers and hanging-baskets that leave the ground area free for other features. Such containers also make gardening possible in courtyards where the ground may be totally paved. Always ensure that these containers are positioned where they cannot drip water on plants below, dribble dirty water down a colour-washed wall, or be knocked by passing heads.

SUCCESS WITH HANGING-BASKETS

- Don't cram masses of plants into one basket. Once established, fewer but bigger and healthier plants look better than a crowd of space-starved plants.
- Don't use too many different types of plants. A dozen totally different plants will not look as effective as 12 plants of only four kinds.
- When planting a hanging-basket, choose a medley of trailing, bushy and upright plants.
- Don't be afraid to try a single-subject basket – they look distinctive and very attractive.
- Try colour variations if you want lots of variety. Mixed colours of the same species give the impression of a very colourful basket without any problem of some plants physically dominating their neighbours and consequently spoiling the entire display.

SINGLE-SUBJECT DISPLAYS

These are increasingly popular and without the risk of dominant plants swamping others. Here are a few displays to consider.

- *Calceolaria integrifolia* **'Sunshine' (Slipper Flower):** half-hardy perennial, creating a 'ball' of yellow (see opposite page).

- **Cascade Geraniums (Continental Geraniums):** half-hardy annuals with masses of flowers in a wide colour range throughout summer (see opposite page).

- *Lobelia erinus* **(Edging and Trailing Lobelia):** half-hardy annual with a bushy or trailing nature, in mixed or single colours (see opposite page).

Anthemis punctata subsp. *cupaniana*
Golden Marguerite (UK/USA)

Also known as *Anthemis cupaniana*, this short-lived herbaceous perennial has masses of daisy-like, white flowers with bright yellow centres from early to late summer. Finely dissected, grey leaves.

Soil and situation: light, loam-based, well-drained soil in full sun and shelter from cold wind.

Increasing plants: remove and divide congested plants in spring, replanting young pieces from around the outside.

↥ 15–20 cm (6–8 in) ↔ 30–38 cm (12–15 in)

Aucuba japonica 'Variegata'
Gold Dust Plant (USA)

Spotted laurel (UK)

Also known as *Aucuba japonica* 'Maculata', this hardy, evergreen shrub has dark green leaves splashed in yellow. It is ideal for growing in a large tub.

Soil and situation: well-drained, moisture-retentive, soil-based compost in light shade or full sun.

Increasing plants: take 10–13 cm (4–5 in) long cuttings from the current season's growth and insert in pots of equal parts moist peat and sharp sand in late summer. Place in a cold frame.

↥ 1–1.2 m (3½–4 ft) ↔ 90 cm–1.2 m (3–4 ft)

Choisya ternata 'Sundance'
Yellow-leaved Mexican Orange Blossom (UK/USA)

Slightly tender, evergreen shrub with golden-yellow leaves and faintly scented white flowers in late spring and early summer, and often intermittently throughout summer.

Soil and situation: well-drained, loam-based compost in full sun and sheltered from cold wind.

Increasing plants: take 7.5 cm (3 in) long cuttings in mid-summer and insert in pots of equal parts moist peat and sharp sand. Place in gentle warmth.

↥ 75 cm–1 m (2½–3½ ft) ↔ 75–90 cm (2½–3 ft)

Clematis macropetala

Slender-stemmed, deciduous and bushy climber with light and dark blue flowers during late spring and early summer. It is spectacular when planted in the top of a large barrel or pot and allowed to trail over the sides.

Soil and situation: fertile, neutral to slightly alkaline, soil-based compost in full sun.

Increasing plants: take 7.5 cm (3 in) long stem-cuttings in mid-summer and insert in pots of equal parts moist peat and sharp sand. Place in gentle warmth.

↔ Trails for 1.5–2.1m (5–7 ft)

Fatsia japonica
False Castor Oil Plant (UK)

Japanese Fatsia (USA)

Slightly tender, evergreen shrub with large, glossy, hand-like leaves. White flowers appear in autumn and often throughout winter.

Soil and situation: light, well-drained but moisture-retentive soil in a tub. Position in light shade or full sun, with shelter from cold wind.

Increasing plants: detach sucker-like shoots in spring and insert in pots of equal parts moist peat and sharp sand. Place in a cold frame.

↕ 1.5–2.1 m (5–7 ft) ↔ 1.5–1.8 m (5–6 ft)

Hebe x andersonii 'Variegata'

Slightly tender, evergreen shrub with cream and green variegated leaves. From mid-summer to early autumn it bears lavender-blue flowers.

Soil and situation: light, well-drained but moisture-retentive loam-based compost in full sun and shelter from cold wind.

Increasing plants: take 7.5 cm (3 in) long cuttings during mid-summer and insert in pots of equal parts moist peat and sharp sand. Place in a cold frame.

↕ 75–90 cm (2½–3 ft) ↔ 60–90 cm (2–3 ft)

Osteospermum ecklonis var. prostratum

African Daisy (UK)

Also known as *Dimorphotheca ecklonis* 'Prostrata', this tender perennial has white-petalled flowers with mustard-yellow centres in mid- and late summer.

Soil and situation: well-drained but moisture-retentive loam-based compost in full sun.

Increasing plants: take 5 cm (2 in) long cuttings from sideshoots in mid-summer and insert in pots of equal parts moist peat and sharp sand in a cold frame.

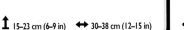

↕ 15–23 cm (6–9 in) ↔ 30–38 cm (12–15 in)

PLANTS FOR HANGING-BASKETS

- *Antirrhinum pendula multiflora* **'Chinese Lanterns':** half-hardy annual with a cascading habit: there are many different colours, as well as bicolours, creating a distinctive feature.
- *Calceolaria integrifolia* **'Sunshine' (Slipper Flower):** half-hardy perennial with a trailing and cascading habit and bright yellow, pouch-like flowers.
- *Campanula isophylla* **(Italian Bellflower/Star of Bethlehem):** hardy perennial with a trailing and cascading habit; it produces masses of star-shaped, blue or white flowers.
- **Cascade Geraniums (Continental Geraniums):** half-hardy annuals with a cascading habit; it bears masses of flowers in shades of scarlet, salmon, pink and lilac. These plants soon saturate a container in colour.
- *Helichrysum petiolare:* half-hardy perennial with long, trailing stems and attractive leaves. There are several forms, some with single-coloured leaves, others variegated.
- *Fuchsia* **(Lady's Eardrops):** tender perennials, many with a cascading habit and ideal as a centrepiece in a hanging-basket. They become awash with distinctive, colourful flowers.
- *Lobelia erinus* **(Edging and Trailing Lobelia):** half-hardy annual with a bushy or trailing habit; it has blue, white or red flowers.
- *Lobularia maritima pendula:* also known as *Alyssum maritimum pendula*, this half-hardy annual has a trailing habit and produces cream, purple, pink, rose and purple flowers.
- *Pelargonium peltatum* **(Trailing or Ivy-leaved Geranium):** tender perennial with a trailing and cascading habit; there are many varieties, in colours including white, pink, salmon, lilac and red.
- *Petunia milliflora* **'Fantasy':** half-hardy annual, with a compact habit and trumpet-shaped flowers in many colours.

Small conifers

Slow-growing and small conifers have many uses, especially in small gardens. Small and upright types, such as *Juniperus communis* 'Compressa' (see below), can be used in winter-flowering windowboxes, and others in tubs and large pots (see below for suitable types). They are also ideal in rock gardens and scree beds, where they create height and miniature focal points among spring-flowering bulbs. They also do well in sink-garden displays.

SLOW-GROWING CONIFERS FOR CONTAINERS

- *Chamaecyparis pisifera* '**Filifera Aurea**': evergreen conifer with a conical outline and spreading branches that are packed with thread-like, golden-yellow foliage. Eventually, it has a mop-like outline.
- *Chamaecyparis lawsoniana* '**Ellwoodii**': evergreen conifer with short, feather-like sprays of grey-green leaves that, in winter, assume shades of steel-blue.
- *Platycladus orientalis* '**Aurea Nana**': also known as *Thuja orientalis* 'Aurea Nana', this hardy, evergreen conifer has a neat, rounded nature and light yellow-green foliage.
- *Thuja plicata* '**Stoneham Gold**': hardy, evergreen conifer with a conical outline and bright, golden foliage with coppery-bronze tips. The foliage remains attractive throughout the dull months of winter.

OTHER SLOW-GROWING AND SMALL CONIFERS

- *Abies balsamea* '**Hudsonia**': hardy, compact and very slow-growing conifer with a flattish top formed of grey leaves that turn mid-green in mid-summer.
  Height: 45–60 cm (1½–2 ft) Spread: 50–60 cm (20–24 in)
- *Chamaecyparis lawsoniana* '**Ellwood's Gold Pillar**': hardy, evergreen, spire-like, slow-growing conifer that is tightly covered with golden-yellow foliage.
  Height: 75–90 cm (2½–3 ft) Spread: 25 cm (10 in)
- *Juniperus communis* '**Compressa**': hardy, slow-growing conifer with a compact, column-like habit and green, silver-backed leaves. It is ideal for planting in a small rock garden, in a miniature garden created in a stone sink or in a scree bed.
  Height: 30–45 cm (1–1½ ft) Spread: 10–15 cm (4–6 in)

Juniperus communis 'Depressa Aurea'

Hardy, spreading, evergreen conifer with slightly feathery, bright yellow foliage in spring and summer, turning bronze by autumn. It is ideal for a large rock garden, or alongside a path where its branches cloak the edges.

Soil and situation: well-drained but moisture-retentive soil in light shade or full sun.

Pruning: no pruning is needed.

↕ 30–38 cm (12–15 in) ↔ 1.2–1.5 m (4–5 ft)

Picea glauca var. albertiana 'Conica'

Also known as *Picea glauca* 'Albertiana Conica', this hardy, slow-growing conifer forms a distinctive conical outline. It is densely packed with soft, grass-green foliage and is especially attractive in spring when new growth appears.

Soil and situation: well-drained soil in full sun.

Pruning: no pruning is needed.

↕ 75–90 cm (2½–3 ft) ↔ 75–90 cm (2½–3 ft)

Taxus baccata 'Standishii'

Also known as *Taxus baccata* 'Fastigiata Standishii', it is hardy, evergreen, slow-growing and columnar. It is tightly packed with golden-yellow leaves and is especially attractive in winter.

Soil and situation: well-drained soil in slight shade or full sun.

Pruning: no pruning is needed.

↕ 1.2–1.5 m (4–5 ft) ↔ 25–30 cm (10–12 in)

Culinary herbs

The range of small-garden herbs is very wide, and they introduce exciting and unusual flavours to vegetables as well as fish and meat dishes; sandwiches and soups also benefit from them. Pots of young herbs are relatively inexpensive to buy and most will last for several years; even then, many can be lifted, divided and replanted. Some herbs, such as Parsley, are raised each year from seeds sown in a sheltered seed bed or a pot.

Which herbs can I grow?

PLACES TO GROW HERBS

- **Containers:** clusters of herbs in pots are convenient for placing near a kitchen door. Additionally, pots help to restrain invasive types such as mints which, in a border, would intrude on neighbouring plants.
- **Cartwheel gardens:** these are often replicated by stones for the rim and spokes, with small herbs planted between them.
- **Chessboard designs:** paving slabs laid in a chessboard (checkerboard) pattern, with clusters of herbs in the spaces. This enables herbs to be easily reached.

OTHER CULINARY HERBS FOR SMALL GARDENS

The range of culinary herbs is wide and includes:
- *Allium schoenoprasum* (**Chives**): hardy perennial with a bulbous nature and grass-like, tubular, mid-green leaves. During early and mid-summer it develops globular heads of rose-pink, starry flowers. The chopped leaves are used to give a mild onion flavour to salads, omelettes and soups.
- *Melissa officinalis* (**Balm**): hardy herbaceous perennial, grown for its lemon-scented, wrinkled-surfaced and somewhat heart-shaped green leaves. The leaves are used fresh or dried in iced drinks and fruit salads.
- *Satureja hortensis* (**Summer Savory**): hardy annual with a bushy nature and spicily flavoured, dark green leaves. They are used to flavour fish, meat and soups, as well as egg and cheese dishes.
- *Thymus vulgaris* (**Thyme**): also known as Common or Garden Thyme, this hardy, low-growing, evergreen shrub has aromatic, dark green leaves. They are used fresh or dried to flavour stuffings, and in fish dishes, casseroles and soups.

Mentha spicata (Common Mint)

Also known as Spearmint, this hardy, herbaceous perennial has aromatic leaves with a distinctive spearmint flavour. They are used in mint sauce and jelly, as well as for flavouring vegetables.

Soil and situation: light, fertile, moisture-retentive but well-drained soil in slight shade and a warm position. It is best grown in containers to restrict its spread.

Increasing plants: lift and divide congested plants in spring; replant young pieces direct in their growing positions.

↕ 38–45 cm (15–18 in)   ↔ Vigorous and invasive

Petroselinum crispum (Parsley)

Hardy biennial invariably grown as an annual. It has branching stems, bearing curly, moss-like, mid-green leaves. It develops greenish-yellow flowers, but these should be removed. Leaves are used to garnish fish dishes and sandwiches, and to flavour sauces.

Soil and situation: light, fertile, well-drained but moisture-retentive soil in light shade or sun.

Increasing plants: sow seeds in shallow drills in an outdoor seed bed from early spring to mid-summer.

↕ 30–45 cm (1–1½ ft)   ↔ 23–38 cm (9–15 in)

Salvia officinalis (Sage)

Slightly tender, evergreen shrub with grey-green, wrinkled, aromatic leaves and tubular, violet-blue flowers during early and mid-summer. The leaves are used to flavour meats and stuffings.

Soil and situation: light, fertile, well-drained but moisture-retentive soil in full sun.

Increasing plants: take 7.5 cm (3 in) long cuttings from the current season's shoots in late summer. Insert them in equal parts moist peat and sharp sand, and place in a cold frame.

↕ 45–60 cm (1½–2 ft)   ↔ 45–60 cm (1½–2 ft)

Fruit: soft and top

Where possible in a small garden, grow tree fruits in borders; perhaps narrow ones alongside walls for warmth-loving types (peaches and nectarines) or in beds alongside paths which give ready access to them. Fruits grown in containers – whether apples or strawberries – need regular attention, especially to ensure that the compost does not become dry. In particular, strawberries in hanging-baskets need regular watering.

PICKING FRUIT

- **Apples and pears:** test for picking by cupping individual fruits and gently lifting and twisting. If the stalk readily parts from the branch, the fruit is ready to be picked.
- **Blackcurrants:** fruits are ready for picking about a week after turning blue-black; those at the top of each strig (bunch) ripen first and can be picked individually.
- **Peaches and nectarines:** pick when the flesh around the stalk is soft; pick in the same way as for apples.
- **Plums:** fruits are ready for picking when they easily part from the tree – the stalk usually remains on the tree. Take care not to squeeze and bruise them.
- **Raspberries:** when fruits are fully coloured but still firm, pull them off; leave the plug attached to the plant.
- **Strawberries:** pick fruits when they are coloured all over. Pick when dry, with the stalk attached to the fruit.

STRAWBERRIES IN CONTAINERS

- **Hanging-baskets:** use a seed-raised variety and buy young plants in late spring or early summer. Put three plants in a large hanging-basket. Do not put baskets outside until all risk of frost has passed.

- **Strawberry planters:** these have cupped holes in their sides in which plants can be placed – as well as in the top. Ensure good drainage; roll a piece of wire-netting (slightly less than the depth of the planter) to form a tube about 7.5 cm (3 in) wide. Insert this into the planter and fill with large stones. Fill the planter with loam-based compost to level with the lowest cupped hole, and put a plant in it. Continue filling and planting; lastly, put plants in the top. Thoroughly water the compost.

Apples
In confined areas, grow apples either as espaliers or cordons against walls, or as dwarf pyramids or dwarf bushes in tubs and large pots. Dwarfing rootstocks such as M27 or M9 are essential, especially for apples in containers. To ensure pollination (and subsequent development of fruit) compatible varieties close by are essential. Where only one tree is possible, choose a 'family' tree, where three or four varieties have been grafted on to it. Additionally, specifically choose varieties for their flavour.

Blackcurrants
Easily grown bush fruits, with shoots growing directly from soil level. Fruits are borne on shoots produced during the previous year – expect a yearly yield of 4.5–6.8 kg (10–15 lb) from each bush. As soon as fruits have been picked, cut out all stems that produced fruits. This leaves young shoots (produced during that season) to bear fruits during the following year. Bushes grow about 1.5 m (5 ft) high and wide, with picking mainly during mid-summer.

Gooseberries
Usually grown as bushes, with fruits borne on a permanent framework of shoots supported by a single, leg-like stem. From a bush – 90 cm–1.5 m (3–5 ft) high – expect a yearly yield of 2.70–5.44 kg (6–12 lb) fruits. Picking time is mainly in mid-summer. Prune established bushes between early winter and early spring, cutting back by half new growth at the ends of stems. Additionally, cut back sideshoots to 5 cm (2 in) long.

Peaches

Succulent fruits with somewhat rough, hairy skin. In a small garden, fan-trained trees are best, positioned against a warm, wind-sheltered wall. From an established fan-trained tree expect a yield of 9 kg (20 lb) when grown on a St Julien A rootstock; space trees 4.5 m (15 ft) apart. For a small garden use Pixy rootstock, with 2.4 m (8 ft) between trees, and expect a yearly yield of 4.5 kg (10 lb) of fruits. Fruits are picked mainly during mid-summer and the early part of late summer.

Pears

In confined areas, grow pears either as espaliers, 4.5 m (15 ft) apart, or cordons, 75 cm (2½ ft) apart. Pollination partners are essential and, in a small garden, the easiest way to overcome this problem is to plant a family tree, where several varieties have been grafted onto the same tree. Fruits are ready for picking (depending on the variety) during late summer and early or mid-autumn, and usually ready for eating some time later. Established espaliers yield 6.8–11.3 kg (15–25 lb) of fruits, while a single cordon 1.8–2.72 kg (4–6 lb).

Raspberries – summer-fruiting types

Popular cane fruits, needing a supporting framework of tiered wires, 30–38 cm (12–15 in) apart to 1.8 m (6 ft) high. These are strained between strong posts and in full sun. Avoid frost-pockets on slopes. Immediately after picking, cut out all fruited canes to ground level and tie in young canes. Fertile, moisture-retentive soil is essential to encourage the yearly production of canes that during the following year bear fruits during mid- and late summer. Expect yields of 2 kg (4½lb) for each 90 cm (3 ft) of row.

Strawberries – summer-fruiting types

Popular soft fruit for growing in beds as well as in containers (see above). Summer-fruiting types are harvested during early and mid-summer, with plants remaining productive for 3–4 years. For a worthwhile crop, you should put at least 20 plants in a bed, and expect a yield of up to 680 g (24 oz) from each plant.

Other types of these fruits include Alpine Strawberries, with a productive life of one year and cropping from mid-summer to autumn. They are best grown in a container.

OTHER FRUITS FOR SMALL GARDENS

- **Blackberries:** popular cane fruit, needing a supporting framework of tiered wires, 30 cm (12 in) apart from 90 cm (3 ft) to 2.1 m (7 ft) high. These are strained between strong posts and in full sun or light shade. Immediately after picking, cut out all fruited canes to ground level and tie in young canes. Fertile, moisture-retentive soil is essential to encourage the yearly production of canes that during the following year bear fruits mainly during late summer and early autumn. Expect yields of 4.5–11.3 kg (10–25 lb) from each plant – spaced 2.4–3.6 m (8–12 ft) apart, depending on vigour.
- **Nectarines:** smooth-skinned form of the peach. There are several varieties, but all less hardy than peaches and therefore best grown as fan-trained trees against a warm, wind-sheltered wall. Grow it on the St Julien A rootstock and expect a yield of 4.5 kg (10 lb) from each fan-trained tree.
- **Raspberries - autumn-fruiting types:** fruits are similar to those of summer-fruiting types (see above), but produce fruits from late summer to mid-autumn. Autumn-fruiting raspberries bear fruits on the tips of shoots produced earlier during the same season and for this reason pruning is easier than for summer-fruiting types. In late winter of each year, cut all canes to ground level; in spring, fresh shoots appear and these bear fruits later in the year. Expect a yield from established plants of about 68 g (1½ lb) for each 90 cm (3 ft) of row. Plants remain productive for 7–10 years, when they start to deteriorate through virus infections.
- **Red currants:** popular fruit, usually grown as a bush and growing 1.5–1.8 m (5-6 ft) high and wide. Bushes have a permanent framework of shoots supported by a single, leg-like stem. From each bush, expect a yearly yield 4.5 kg (10 lb). Bushes remain productive for 10–15 years. Picking time is usually mid-summer, although some varieties are not ready until the early part of late summer.
- **White currants:** grown in the same way as red currants (with a similar yield), and both also can be grown as single, double or triple cordons.

Vegetables

Are vegetables possible on a balcony?

By growing small, summer-only vegetables in containers it is possible to have fresh food on a balcony. Herbs in pots are other candidates. Cold, windswept balconies can be made more hospitable for plants by attaching clear plastic to the balustrade. Hot, sun-drenched balconies also can be a problem for plants, which then need further regular watering. A hanging-basket with tomatoes is a possibility, especially in sheltered positions.

VEGETABLES IN GROWING-BAGS

Several vegetables grow well in growing-bags on a sheltered patio or balcony. Plant as soon as all risk of frost has passed.

- **Bush French beans:** plant six bushy plants. The pods are ready to be picked when they snap if bent – usually when they are around 10–15 cm (4–6 in) long.
- **Courgettes:** use two plants. Water and feed plants regularly and harvest them while young and tender. This encourages the development of further courgettes.
- **Lettuces:** grow eight lettuces in a bag.
- **Potatoes:** in early to mid-spring cut eight 7.5–10 cm (3–4 in) long cross-slits in the top and push a tuber of an early variety of potato into each. Cover them, water them and fold back the plastic to exclude light.

TOMATOES IN CONTAINERS

- **Hanging-baskets:** use a 45 cm (18 in) wide, wire-framed basket and line with polythene. Partly fill with equal parts soil-based and peat-based compost; when all risk of frost has passed, plant a bush-type variety such as 'Tumbler'. Use a knife to slit small holes in the polythene; then, water the compost. Plants are naturally bushy and do not need to have sideshoots removed.

- **Growing-bags:** plant 3–4 'cordon' types in a growing-bag. Supports are essential (proprietary types are available). Regularly water and feed plants. Remove sideshoots and regularly pick fruits when ripe.

- **Pots:** plant a 'cordon' type in a large pot of loam-based compost. Support the plant with a cane. Remove sideshoots.

Beetroot

Choose Globe Beetroot, which are round and quick maturing and include 'Burpee's Golden' (superb flavour, with yellow flesh) and 'Detroit' (red flesh; stores well).

Sowing: in spring, shallowly fork soil and rake to a fine tilth. Form drills 2.5 cm (1 in) deep and 30 cm (12 in) apart. Sow in clusters of 2–3 seeds, 10–15 cm (4–6 in) apart. Thin seedlings to one at each position.

Harvesting: insert a garden fork under roots and gently lift without bruising the globes. Twist off the leaves.

Carrots

Choose Short-rooted Carrots (which are finger-like) or those that resemble small golf balls; these include 'Amsterdam Forcing' (early variety with stump-end roots) and 'Parmex' (round, and ideal for containers as well as vegetable beds).

Sowing: from mid-spring to the latter part of early summer, sow seeds in drills 12–18 mm (½–¾ in) deep and 15 cm (6 in) apart. Sow thinly and thin seedlings to about 6 cm (2½ in) apart. Refirm soil around remaining seedlings.

Harvesting: When young carrots are large enough to be eaten, pull them up. Twist off foliage, just above the roots.

French beans

These are ideal for small gardens, as well as wind-exposed positions. Choose varieties such as 'Masterpiece' (flat pods), 'Tendergreen' (pencil podded) and 'The Prince' (flat pods).

Sowing: fertile, moisture-retentive soil is essential to ensure rapid growth. In late spring or early summer, form drills 5 cm (2 in) deep and 45 cm (18 in) apart. Sow individual seeds 7.5–10 cm (3–4 in) apart.

Harvesting: from mid-summer onwards, pick the pods when young; they should snap when bent sideways. Regular picking encourages the development of further beans.

Lettuces

There are several types of lettuce.

- **Cabbage types:** includes Butterheads (soft-leaved and globular) and Crispheads (round and crisp heads).
- **Cos types:** upright, with crisp, oblong heads. They take longer to grow than cabbage types, and they are slightly more difficult.
- **Loose-leaf types:** they do not develop a heart; instead, each plant has masses of leaves that can be harvested individually. This type is ideal for a small garden and where only a few leaves are needed at one time.

Radishes

Choose summer radishes, such as 'Cherry Belle' (globular), 'French Breakfast' (oblong), 'Juliette' (globular), 'Red Prince' (globular) and 'Scarlet Globe' (globular).

Sowing: from mid-spring to late summer sow seeds every two weeks. Form drills 12 mm (½ in) deep and 15 cm (6 in) apart and sow thinly. When the seedlings are large enough to handle, thin them 2.5 cm (1 in) apart.

Harvesting: pull up young plants when large enough to be used in salads.

Spring onions

Also known as salad onions and bunching onions, spring onions are ideal for adding to salads. Choose varieties such as 'White Lisbon' and 'Ishikuro'.

Sowing: dig the soil in winter and in early spring fork and rake it to create a fine tilth. Every two weeks from early or mid-spring to the early part of mid-summer, sow seeds in drills 12 mm (½ in) deep and 10–13 cm (4–5 in) apart. This produces onions from early summer to early autumn.

Harvesting: use a garden fork to loosen soil and pull up the plants.

Tomatoes

Popular fruit for growing outdoors in containers (see above). There are two main types.

- **Cordon varieties:** supported by canes or a proprietary framework. Remove all sideshoots and snap off the top of the main stem at a position above the second leaf above the fourth truss (cluster of fruits).
- **Bush varieties:** these need little attention – no removal of sideshoots or the growing tip. Such varieties are ideal for growing in hanging-baskets.

OTHER VEGETABLES FOR SMALL GARDENS

- **Aubergines:** also known as Egg Plants, these frost-tender plants can be grown outdoors in sheltered and warm beds, as well as in growing-bags, large pots, wall-baskets and mangers. Fertile compost is essential; buy established plants and plant as soon as all risk of frost has passed.
- **Beetroot:** choose Globe types, which are round and quick-maturing. During spring, form drills 2.5 cm (1 in) deep and 30 cm (12 in) apart. Sow seeds in clusters of three, 10–15 cm (4–6 in) apart. When the seedlings have formed their first leaves (other than the original seed leaves), thin them to one seedling at each position.
- **Courgettes:** these are frost-tender plants resembling small marrows. They can be grown outdoors in fertile, moisture-retentive soil in full sun, or in growing-bags, wall-baskets and mangers. Plant when all risk of frost has passed and harvest when 10 cm (4 in) long.
- **Cucumbers (outdoor):** also known as ridge cucumbers, they need a warm, sunny, wind-sheltered position. In mid-spring, dig a hole 30 cm (12 in) deep and 38 cm (15 in) wide. Fill it with a mixture of friable soil and well decomposed garden compost. Replace the excavated soil to form a mound. In mid- or late spring in warm areas, or early summer in cold regions, sow three seeds 18 mm (¾ in) deep in a small cluster. Water them and cover with a large jam jar. When seedlings have several leaves, thin them to leave the strongest. Harvest the ripe cucumbers during mid- and late summer, when they are 15–20 cm (6–8 in) long.
- **Runner beans:** where space is short, grow these beans on wigwam of poles 1.8–2.1 m (6–7 ft) high. Erect the supports and in late spring sow 2–3 seeds around the base of each pole. Thin the seedlings to one strong plant for each pole. Harvest the pods while still young and tender, since aged pods tend to become tough and stringy.

Choosing a path

Whatever a garden's size, an all-weather path is essential; it needs to be a fundamental part of a garden's design and not something added as an afterthought. Paths enable easy access to functional features, such as sheds and greenhouses, as well as to more ornamental designs such as summerhouses, gazebos and pergolas. The range of surfaces and material is wide. Some have a rustic charm, while formal ones are better for modern houses and gardens.

Is a garden path necessary?

PATH ESSENTIALS

Apart from having an all-weather surface, the design of a path should:
• unite all parts of a garden;
• create a visual perspective, so that the eye is not confused and has a known feature to travel along;
• introduce style, whether formal or informal; and
• be individualist and unique, creating originality.

PLANNING THE ROUTE

Informal garden

Following a flower border | Leading to a focal point | Around a feature

Formal garden

Leading to a feature | To a gate or archway | A walk around the garden

RANGE OF PATHS

There is a great variety of path materials and many ways to use them. Below and on the opposite page are many inspirational designs. Some are suitable for informal gardens, whereas others are more clinical and formal. Always select a style that harmonizes with your garden planting and does not confuse the eye.

↗ *Gravel paths edged with lavender are ideal for an informal garden.*

↗ *Paving slabs in several sizes help to create a semi-formal path.*

↗ *Bricks or pavers in a herringbone pattern look tidy and attractive.*

↗ *Complex patterns using paving slabs and bricks give an exotic touch.*

↗ *Crazy paving is suitable for a relaxed garden atmosphere.*

↗ *Ribbed-surface concrete paths are slip resistant and easy to build.*

CORNERS, CURVES AND STEPS

Square paving slabs are useful for path construction as well as steps.

Curved paths rather than straight ones are better suited to an informal area.

When selecting a path, always consider whether materials used in its construction are able to cope with curves. Some materials, such as square paving slabs, are best used on straight paths, whereas crazy paving is suitable for both straight and curved areas.

PATH EDGING

Log rolls are relatively inexpensive to buy and are easy to install.

Ornate path edgings help to create a unique and exciting garden.

Tough house bricks or pavers set at an angle have an informal air.

Edgings formed of log rolls or bricks set at an angle are ideal for curved paths, whereas concrete edging slabs and bricks when laid flat are difficult to negotiate around a curve. Some edgings can be used to abut a lawn, but side constraints are essential where a path is formed of gravel.

MORE PATH DESIGNS

The range of designs for paths is wide, and further ones to consider are featured here. Some have a formal nature. Informal ones are ideal for cottage gardens. Before making any decisions about a path, look around other gardens.

↗ *Cobble paths, with bricks installed at their edges, are easy to lay.*

↗ *Coloured setts can be laid in complex patterns in an ornate garden.*

↗ *Bricks laid crossways may look attractive but they are not very strong.*

↗ *Use stone chippings for rustic paths, edging them to retain the stones.*

↗ *Old pieces of paving introduce an informal style to a garden.*

↗ *Wooden strips with pea gravel between them are very eye-catching.*

DEALING WITH TOPSOIL

Light, friable topsoil (to a depth of about 23 cm/9 in depending on the area) is ideal for spreading on soil in shrub borders.

DEALING WITH SUBSOIL

Heavy subsoil is invariably mostly formed of clay and without a great deal of initial benefit to young plants in a garden. Therefore, it is best tipped into a rubbish skip ready for disposal.

Slopes and paths to avoid

The construction materials for some paths are not suitable for slopes, where the surface is uneven and undulating.

Paths to avoid on a slope are those:
- formed of gravel or pea shingle that spills on to other areas;
- with large paving slabs that would, at their joints, be uneven; and
- formed of flexible pavers laid on a bed of sharp sand.

Reconstituted stone slabs framed with cast 'Celtic' pavers. There are many such pavers on the market.

Square pavers when laid diagonally and with slabs cut into triangles for positioning along the sides create unusual patterns. Use bricks to form ornamental yet functional edgings.

Well-weathered bricks create paths with an aged appearance and are ideal for informal and cottage-type gardens. Ensure that the bricks are laid on a strong, secure base.

Path construction

Which is the best material for a path?

For straight paths, use materials such as paving slabs and concrete pavers which will not need cutting and trimming. These are also best used on flat surfaces. Conversely, for a meandering path on sloping ground, choose crazy paving. Natural stone is also a possibility, but is more expensive. Because plants are often planted in the spaces between pieces of natural stone, do not use a spade to clear snow and ice away, nor put salt on the path.

LAYING PAVING SLABS

Pre-cast paving slabs are ideal for creating a firm, all-weather surface. They can be used on their own or combined with other materials, such as bricks, to create decorative patterns.

Step 1
Prepare the area of the path by removing topsoil and adding a 10 cm (4 in) thick layer of compacted hardcore.

Step 2
Spread and level a 5–7.5 cm (2–3 in) thick layer of sharp sand over the compacted hardcore.

Step 3
Mark on the sand the area of the first slab and place five blobs of mortar on it – one in each corner and one in the centre.

Step 4
Carefully place a paving slab in position and check that it has a gentle slope so that surface water drains away.

Step 5
Position the next slab and check its slope. If the slabs have straight edges, place 12 mm (½ in) thick spaces between them.

Step 6
When the mortar is hard, remove the spaces and fill the joints with a stiff, dry, weak mortar mix (see below).

CUTTING PAVING SLABS

It is often necessary to cut paving slabs. Professionals use powered cutters (angle-grinders), but home gardeners can use a bolster (type of cold chisel) and a club hammer. Wear goggles and strong gloves and score a line on the slab (all edges and sides). Then, using the bolster and club hammer, work around the slab, several times. When complete, place the slab on a board, so that the scored line is positioned above its edge. Use the wooden handle of a clump hammer to knock the slab sharply so it breaks along the line.

WHEN FILLING JOINTS

When filling gaps between paving slabs, take care that the mixture does not go on top of them, as it leaves marks. Instead, line the edges with masking tape; then use a stiff, dry, weak mortar mixture to fill the gaps. Ram this level, to just below the surfaces of the slabs.

Cutting concrete brick pavers

Unless a squared pattern (see right) is used to lay pavers, cutting is essential. This can be done by using a bolster chisel and club hammer in the same way as for paving slabs (see above, right); when laying a large patio it is better to hire a hydraulic stone splitter. Don't forget to wear goggles and strong gloves.

LAYING CONCRETE PAVERS

Also known as 'flexible' pavers, they gain this name because they are laid on a bed of sharp sand and can, if necessary, later be lifted and relaid. They are about the size of house bricks and ideal for straight paths. Crazy paving is better for curved paths.

Step 1
Mark out the area of the path, remove topsoil and install 15 cm (6 in) deep side constraints. These are vital to hold the sand and bricks in place.

Step 2
Spread and firm a 7.5 cm (3 in) thick layer of hardcore over the base.

Step 3
Spread a 5 cm (2 in) thick layer of sharp sand over the hardcore. Select a 15 cm (6 in) deep piece of timber; cut notches at the ends so that when drawn over the sand it leaves the surface the thickness of the paver, minus 9 mm (⅜ in), below the top of the sides.

Step 4
Place the pavers on the sand in the desired pattern (see right).

Step 5
Compact the pavers by placing a flat piece of wood on the surface and repeatedly tapping it with a club hammer.

Step 6
Brush sharp sand over the surface, then again compact the pavers. Repeat this, then water the surface with a fine-rosed watering-can.

CONSTRUCTING A GRAVEL PATH

Gravel or pea-shingle paths have a relaxing ambience, yet can be either formal or informal depending on the edging. Strong side constraints are essential. Provide these with concrete slabs or strong wood.

Warning: If cats are likely to dig up the surface, use a thin layer of pea-shingle over gravel.

1 *Dig out the area of the path, 10 cm (4 in) deep and 90 cm–1.2 m (3–4 ft) wide. Ensure that the path is dug out to an even depth, especially along its edges.*

2 *Position concrete side constraints, 90 cm (3 ft) long, 5 cm (2 in) thick and 15 cm (6 in) deep. Use a spirit level to check that the sides are level. Cement them in place.*

Stepping trunks!

Section of a wide log

Gravel paths can be made more attractive by letting sections of wide tree trunks into them. A piece of wire netting secured on top of each slice prevents them becoming slippery.

3 *When the side constraints are firm and cannot be moved, use a sledge hammer or club hammer to break up large bricks to form an even base. Do not dislodge the side constraints.*

4 *Spread pea shingle over the rubble, so that its surface is about 2.5 cm (1 in) below the side constraints. Use a short piece of stout wood or a metal garden rake.*

PATTERNS FOR PAVERS

Complex patterns are best left to professional constructors. Several bonds are simple to create, including running and basketweave.

Before deciding the path's width, lay out pavers on a flat surface to the desired pattern. The width of the path can then be tailored to suit this measurement, thereby avoiding any unnecessary cutting of pavers.

Basketweave bond

Running bond (crosswise)

Running bond (lengthwise)

Herringbone bond

Squared bond

Simple bond with cross pavers

Constructing a crazy-paving path

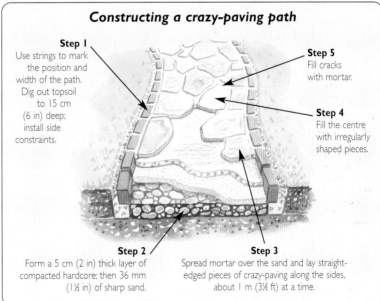

Step 1 Use strings to mark the position and width of the path. Dig out topsoil to 15 cm (6 in) deep; install side constraints.

Step 5 Fill cracks with mortar.

Step 4 Fill the centre with irregularly shaped pieces.

Step 2 Form a 5 cm (2 in) thick layer of compacted hardcore; then 36 mm (1½ in) of sharp sand.

Step 3 Spread mortar over the sand and lay straight-edged pieces of crazy-paving along the sides, about 1 m (3½ ft) at a time.

LAYING A NATURAL STONE PATH

Natural stone forms attractive paths. Use strings to mark the path's area and dig out topsoil. Add hardcore, then 5 cm (2 in) of sharp sand. Because of its uneven thickness, natural stone is more difficult to lay than crazy paving. Lay the stones on blobs of mortar. Dig out sand and hardcore from some of the larger joints, and fill with soil-based compost. Later, small, prostrate plants can be put in them.

Making a patio

Is a patio necessary in a small garden?

In a small garden, an all-weather patio is essential, especially as it may be the main area for growing plants. Clusters of pots and tubs, as well as summer flowers burgeoning from windowboxes, wall-baskets and hanging-baskets (see pages 26–27), create magnificent displays. The patio's surface must be well drained and the base firm. You should also design the patio to complement the overall garden style (see pages 20–33 for a range of gardens).

Reconstituted stone slabs in various sizes can be laid in informal patterns.

A combination of strong decking and raised beds produces an unusual patio area.

Bricks laid in a semi-circle create an attractive and unusual patio area.

DESIGN CONSIDERATIONS

- **Awnings:** where a patio faces strong sunlight, consider installing a large, retractable awning. It may need to be taken down in autumn and stored in a dry shed.
- **Large parasols:** these can be attached to tables or used as free-standing features secured to a firm base and angled to keep off excessive sun.
- **Steps:** if the garden is at a higher or lower level than the patio, plan to have a series of steps linking them. Also consider a ramp for wheelchair access.
- **Parapets:** where the patio and garden are at different levels, a parapet about 60–75 cm (2–2½ ft) high is essential.

DECKING

Decking has become extremely popular, especially where radically sloping land around a house makes the construction of a door-level patio difficult (see page 69).

Patio material options

↗ Natural stone
Natural stone creates informal patios (see page 63 for laying a path). For larger areas, set them on a thick concrete base.

↗ Paving slabs
Ideal for formal, square and rectangular patios. Half- and quarter-slabs can be introduced for a less clinical design.

↗ Concrete pavers
These have a modern look and can be laid in attractive patterns (see page 63), rather than in clinical rows.

↗ Crazy paving
Informal and ideal for curved patios. It is also able to create gentle slopes, as it easily adapts to differing ground levels.

↗ Granite setts
Create hardwearing and decorative surfaces for informal areas. Individual setts are laid in rounded or straight patterns.

↗ Pebble combinations
Handsome and unusual informal patios can be created from medleys of stones in radial patterns, with cobbles in the spaces.

Design variations

↗ Patterns and modules
Irregular patterns create interest, but they can also confuse the eye.

↗ Different colours
Multi-coloured designs are eye-catching, but can be too dominant.

↗ Material combinations
Medleys of materials with strikingly different colours need careful planning.

↗ Shape combinations
Combinations of different shapes can create distinctive and attractive features.

↗ Split levels
Split-level designs are ideal for uniting a garden on a slope.

PREPARING THE SITE

Shape and size
The length of a patio is usually that of the house. However, if a fence is to be erected between the side of the patio and boundary, leave a 38 cm (15 in) space for posts and construction work. The width needs to harmonize with the building – 3–3.6 m (10–12 ft) for a bungalow, but wider for a house.

Topsoil
Remove topsoil from the planned patio area and scatter it on shrub borders or parts of the garden yet to be created – perhaps an area reserved for a lawn.

Edging boards
Install strong edging boards to mark the patio's area. These will also prevent foundation materials spreading sideways and weakening the surface.

Pegs and levels
When preparing the site, use a series of stout pegs driven into the ground, on top of which a straight piece of wood can be positioned. Place a builder's spirit-level on the board and take readings from several positions. An even fall of 2.5 cm (1 in) in 1.8 m (6 ft) is about right. Ensure that patio surfaces are below the building's damp-proof course.

Slope and drainage
Check that the patio will be sufficiently sloped, so that water readily drains away from the house.

Foundations
A strong, firm base is essential. Usually, 10 cm (4 in) of clean, compacted hardcore is sufficient as a base, but in areas of clay increase this to 15 cm (6 in). Over this spread 5–7.5 cm (2–3 in) of sharp sand. Paving slabs (laid on dabs of fresh mortar) as well as 'flexible' concrete pavers can be laid on top. On soft ground, a 7.5–10 cm (3–4 in) thick layer of concrete can be laid on top of the hardcore to reduce the risk of subsidence.

Planting pockets
Large patios benefit from 1–2 paving slabs left out and the area planted with small shrubs or conifers. Slightly build up the edges of the planting pocket to prevent soil spilling out.

Raised beds
These are larger than planting pockets and with sides 30–45 cm (1–1½ ft) high. Do not position a raised bed in the patio's centre, but towards one side and where it can be easily walked around to admire and look after the plants.

PATIO FEATURES

Apart from constructing an attractive base that harmonizes with the style of garden, patios can be further brightened by adding wall features and simple sculptures. Walls alongside patios create shelter from the wind and make good backdrops for leisure features. Screen-block walling is attractive and instead of presenting a solid wall enables wind to filter through. Tall screen-block walling is not suitable for boundaries, but ideal for separating a major part of a garden from a patio.

→ *Wall-mounted water features create added interest. Here, a lion's head is surrounded by a large-flowering clematis, with water trickling into an old container.*

Choosing a fence

Why have a fence?

Long gone are the days when a front garden needed a fortress-like perimeter. Yet an attractive fence, with a style compatible with the house, helps to mark territory and to deter dogs from entering. Select gates that harmonize with the fence, with rustic types for informal perimeter arches drenched with climbers such as *Lonicera* (Honeysuckle). Gates are used several times a day, and therefore need regular checking for wear and tear.

Fence types

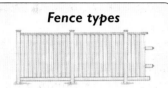

↗ Closeboarded
Vertical pieces of wood nailed to arris rails secured to posts

↗ Horizontal lap panel
Panels, usually 1.8 m (6 ft) long, nailed to strong posts

↗ Interwoven panel
Strips of wood woven to form a panel about 1.8 m (6 ft) long

↗ Wattle fencing
Flexible branches woven to form a panel about 1.8 m (6 ft) long

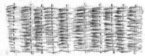

↗ Picket fencing
Vertical strips nailed to horizontal rails secured to posts

↗ Ranch style
Wide boards, usually painted white, screwed to strong posts

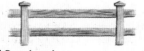

DIY FENCING

Many types of fencing are easily constructed by garden DIY enthusiasts, especially panelled types. Close-boarded fences – where posts support arris rails to which vertical, overlapping timbers are nailed – are slightly more complicated to construct, but not impossible.

COPING WITH SLOPES

Erecting fencing on slopes needs care if the fence is to look professional. With panel fencing, all supporting posts must be upright and panels horizontal, not following ground contours. For close-boarded fencing, supporting posts are upright, with arris rails following the contours but with overlapping timbers nailed vertically on them.

CAPPINGS AND BEVELS

To prevent a post decaying through water entering its top, use two 36 mm (1½ in) long galvanized nails to secure a capping to each post. Alternatively, bevel the top of each supporting post.

Repairing fences

There are many proprietary fixtures for repairing fences, from replacement bases to posts, to repairs to arris rails and fixings for panel fencing.

INCREASING THE HEIGHT OF A FENCE

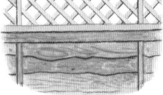

Fences in back gardens – which are perhaps 1.5 m (5 ft) high – can be given added height by securing a piece of lattice-work trellis all along the top.

GATES

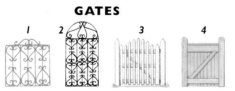

The range of gates is wide, in wood or metal. (1) Wrought-iron gates, perhaps 90 cm (3 ft) high, are ideal for front gardens. There are many patterns and ornamentation. (2) Tall wrought-iron gates are best restricted to side entrances alongside buildings. (3) Picket gates are essential for picket fences. They have a relaxed and informal character. (4) Close-boarded gates are ideal for entrances in leafy hedges, such as those formed of Privet and Yew.

Anti-theft gates

Wrought-iron gates usually have peg hinges. When securing them to a post, position the lower one with the peg upwards to support the gate. Position the upper peg downwards to prevent theft.

Self-closing gates

Proprietary, spring-like devices are available to ensure that gates close each time after use.

Choosing a wall

The life expectancy of a wall mainly depends on the depth of foundations and the type of soil. Shallow foundations and clay soil – especially with the onset of drier and warmer summers – soon cause a wall to tilt and collapse. A capping along the top, to prevent water entering the bricks and freezing, is absolutely essential. This capping must harmonize with the style of the wall. Thick walls usually last longer than single-brick types.

How long will a wall last?

Types of wall

Some are formal in nature and create a solid screen, while others, such as screen-block walling, can be seen through.

↗ **Brick wall**
Formed of regularly sized bricks, these can be laid one or two bricks thick, and in varying bonds (patterns).

↗ **Imitation-stone wall**
Square or rectangular pieces of imitation stone are laid to create an informal-looking wall.

↗ **Dry-stone wall**
Made of natural, irregularly shaped (expensive) stones; alternatively, you can use precast stone pieces.

↗ **Screen-block walling**
Ornamental blocks, 30 cm (12 in) square and 10 cm (4 in) thick, are laid in various decorative patterns.

↗ **Reconstituted stone**
Some having just one ornamental 'face', these 'stones' can create a strong and attractive wall.

↗ **Brick retaining wall**
Formal in nature, and two bricks thick, this is used for holding up a bank of earth; drainage holes are essential.

POINTS TO CONSIDER

Style
Select a style of wall that harmonizes with the rest of the garden.

Height and piers
Walls must be strongly constructed, with piers for high ones. Single-brick thick walls over 75 cm (2½ ft) high need piers every 1.8 m (6 ft). Double-thickness brick walls over 1.2 m (4 ft) high need piers every 1.8–2.4 m (6–8 ft). In areas with strong, gusting winds, reduce the pier spacings. Screen-block walling needs piers, at both ends (if not connected to a wall) and then every 2.4–3 m (8–10 ft).

Foundations
The depths of foundations and thickness of hardcore depends on the wall's height. For up to chest height, 10 cm (4 in) of compacted hardcore and 15 cm (6 in) of concrete is suitable. Over this height, increase the concrete to 20 cm (8 in).

Wall foundation

DRY-STONE WALLS

Unlike brick retaining walls (see above), these have a relaxed look. To assist in soil retention, the wall needs to be battered (leaning and angled backwards). Drainage holes through the wall are essential, as well as a wide area of drainage material behind it.

Battered wall (leaning backwards)

Laying bricks

Laying bricks is an age-old craft and based on the fact that mortar – a mixture of soft sand and cement or lime (or a mixture of both) – bonds one brick with another. Use a mixture of 1 part cement to 3 of soft sand.

Bricklaying

LOW-EDGING WALLS

Double walls, with 25–30 cm (10–12 in) between them, are ideal alongside a patio. Construct them 15–23 cm (6–9 in) high with decorative cappings on top. Top up the area between them with well-drained, friable soil; ideal for summer-flowering bedding plants, or Tulips and biennials for spring displays.

Garden steps

Well-proportioned steps act as a link between two levels and have a unifying influence. The proportions of steps must be attractive as well as easy to use. Usually, the riser (vertical distance) is about 13 cm (5 in) high and the tread 30–38 cm (12–15 in), with an overhang at the front of each step of about 36 mm (1½ in). For some steps, the tread is narrower and the riser up to 20 cm (8 in), but long flights are difficult to negotiate.

TYPES OF STEPS

↗ Free-standing steps
Built between one level and another and keyed into the upper one to give the feature stability. The edges also need to be enclosed by strong walls.

↗ Cut-in steps
Built into a slope or bank, with the flight of steps usually assuming the same angle. Strong foundations are essential; for ease of construction, it is best to use paving slabs.

↗ Decking steps
Use decking steps to change levels within a garden, or to unite decking around a house with the garden. Always use strong timber that has been treated with a wood preservative.

↗ Grass steps
For formal and informal gardens. In formal areas, wide treads of grass with bricks as risers and part treads are attractive; informal areas are better with logs as risers.

↗ Sleepers and gravel
Use railway sleepers to contain treads formed of gravel. Ensure that the sleepers are well secured, with the gravel's surface slightly below their top edges.

BASE STONES

Rather than allowing a lawn to abut a flight of steps, concrete a row of slabs along the base. This will make grass-cutting simpler, as well as making the steps easier to use. Ensure that the base stones are level with the lawn.

COMBINATIONS OF MATERIALS

Using several different types of construction material helps to create greater 'eye appeal'. Consider medleys of paving slabs and bricks (a range of different coloured ones are available).

HANDRAILS

These may be essential for easy walking on steep steps; ensure that they are secure and at elbow height. Metal and wooden ones can be installed (preferably during construction).

RAMPS

In many gardens, sloping paths are essential for easy access. Sloped grass paths, perhaps with stepping stones down the centre, are inexpensive, while combinations of paving slabs and bricks create functional, all-weather surfaces. Do not use shingle or gravel on steep slopes.

PLANTERS

These can be constructed alongside steps, or be flattened positions for plants in containers.

HOW TO MAKE LOG STEPS

Use logs with a uniform thickness – 10–15 cm (4–6 in) – and cut to the width of the path. Excavate the stepped areas, at least 45 cm (18 in) long, and use stout pegs to hold the logs in place. Spread a layer of gravel over the tread areas.

STEP TERMINOLOGY

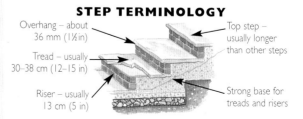

Overhang – about 36 mm (1½ in)

Tread – usually 30–38 cm (12–15 in)

Riser – usually 13 cm (5 in)

Top step – usually longer than other steps

Strong base for treads and risers

Where there is a long flight of steps, you should always include a landing (larger than a step) in the flight.

Decking

Raised decking – constructed on a strong and durable wooden framework supported by wooden or concrete posts cemented into the ground – is a good option for sloping ground or where you have to work over drains and old foundations. Alternatively, decking tiles can be laid on sharp sand at ground level. This is a quick way to create a surface and is sometimes used around 'raised' swimming pools formed from a suspended flexible liner.

Why should I have decking?

ADVANTAGES OF DECKING

Raised decking is more than an elevated patio, attached to a house or free-standing, and as a feature within a garden. It can be built by the side of a pond – or even over it – as well as over inhospitable ground that needs labour-intensive and expensive reclamation.

ELEVATED AND ATTACHED

Most decking is elevated, attached to a house and especially useful where ground falls away dramatically from the house. Elevated decking in such a position needs built-in steps; if they are constructed at the side, this often avoids the cost of long and expensive steps positioned at the front and where the height difference is greatest.

RAISED DECKING

Moderately raised decking within a garden, either centrally or, perhaps, to one corner, creates an attractive feature, but avoid producing high decking that resembles a bandstand and dominates the rest of the garden.

BALUSTRADES

A balustrade of either wood or ornamental wrought iron is essential, especially where raised decking overhangs water or is on a steep slope. Wooden balusters and main supporting posts are usually integral with the design, while metal types are screwed into position later.

DECKING IDEAS

Colourful tiles   *Split-level*   *Verandah*   *Stream-side decking*

ECONOMY DECKING

Decking, especially when formed of multilevel designs, is expensive and time-consuming to construct. An alternative way is to use breeze blocks that are half-buried in the ground and with their surfaces at a uniform height. The breeze blocks can be cemented into the ground. Position 3 m (10 ft) long and 10 cm (4 in) square fencing posts on top, secure them to the breeze blocks and nail pressure-treated gravel boards on top, with spaces between them.

MATERIALS

Use Western Red Cedar or wood that has been pressure-treated with a wood preservative. Brick, concrete or wood (or a combination of them) is essential for supporting piers, while the decking is secured to the joist by galvanized or brass screws with their heads countersunk into the wood. Leave a 6–12 mm (¼–½ in) gap between the planks so that water rapidly drains.

TILE ALTERNATIVES

As an alternative to planks, use 60 cm (2 ft) square timber tiles; space the timber framework so that the tiles are supported along their edges and centres. Tiles can be laid to create attractive patterns, rather than with the slats in a straight line.

PLANK PATTERNS

Straight   *45°*   *Chevron*   *Herringbone*   *Diamond*

TREE SEAT

Where a large, long-trunked, decorative tree is within the proposed area of decking, integrate it into the design; lay decking planks around it and encircle it with a wooden seat.

Winter maintenance

Where decking is in shade and water rests on the surface, it is inevitable that algae will cover the wood and make it unsightly as well as slippery. Use an algicide to remove it.

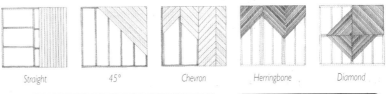

Terraces and verandahs

What are terraces and verandahs?

Many bungalows and houses have a flat, all-weather surface at their rear which forms an outdoor leisure area. Correctly, a terrace is an open area, usually now paved but earlier grassed, that connects a house with a garden. It usually has a balustrade or low wall, especially if raised above the general level of garden. Verandahs are radically different in nature, and the name has an Indian origin, meaning an open-sided gallery around a house.

FORMAL TERRACES

Inevitably, these are covered with paving slabs or companion materials such as bricks in attractive designs. Brick or reconstituted stone balusters and ornate copings create an aged appearance. They have a clinical appearance that sympathizes with many houses, both modern and early 1900s.

INFORMAL TERRACES

These have a relaxed feel, covered in either natural stone paving or reconstituted paving slabs with an old and weathered appearance. Occasionally, grass is used, but only where an all-weather surface is not important and the area is extremely large, so this is not really suitable for a small garden. Informal terraces look good alongside a lawn, where together they create an open-natured feature.

RAISED POND

If a terraced area is large, consider the construction of a raised pond; it is less easy to fall into than a ground-level pond – and the fish and plants are more easily seen.

Pergolas and trellises

These are ideal for integrating onto a terrace that in summer becomes drenched with sun for most of the day. For summer leisure, the shade these features provide will be essential.

Brick pillars on either side of a path's entrance onto a terrace add distinction and highlight the path's position.

VERANDAHS

The term verandah describes a gallery at ground level, on one side or completely surrounding a bungalow or house. They are a real delight, enabling a garden to be taken right up to a house. Most verandahs have a sloping roof. The balustrade is usually of wood to harmonize with the rest of the verandah. Few houses are now built with a verandah and perhaps the feature nearest in design is decking.

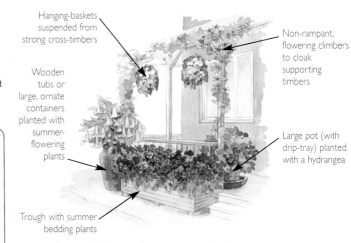

Hanging-baskets suspended from strong cross-timbers

Non-rampant, flowering climbers to cloak supporting timbers

Wooden tubs or large, ornate containers planted with summer-flowering plants

Large pot (with drip-tray) planted with a hydrangea

Trough with summer bedding plants

Verandahs are ideal for merging a garden with a house. In summer, they can be drenched in colour from climbers, bedding plants and small shrubs.

Patios and courtyards

We owe the term patio to the Spaniards, who used it to describe an inner court, open to the sky and surrounded by the dwelling. A patio was an integral part of a house, with walls providing shade. Water features were included to create coolness throughout the year. Nowadays, patio means any paved area. Originally, courtyards were also surrounded by buildings, perhaps inside a castle. Nowadays, courtyard means any area surrounded by walls.

What are patios and courtyards?

PATIO GARDENS

Seclusion and privacy were essential elements for traditional, cloistered patios, although nowadays they are usually open on most aspects. Many types of shrubs, small trees, conifers and bamboos are ideal for growing in tubs and pots, with summer-only plants in hanging-baskets and windowboxes (see pages 26–27). Water features are another consideration for a patio garden, because the repetitive but changing sound of water has a calming, relaxing quality.

Hanging-baskets and tubs are perfect for bringing welcome colour to a bland courtyard wall.

COURTYARD GARDENS

Courtyard gardens mainly rely on plants in containers or, if border space is available at the bases of walls, climbers. Some climbing Roses have a floriferous yet hardy nature, and these include 'Albéric Barbier' (yellow flowers) and 'Zéphirine Drouhin' (fragrant and deep rose-pink flowers).

Fatsia japonica (False Castor Oil Plant – see below)

Tall, ornamental, wrought-iron gate

Large, terracotta pot

Hard, all-weather surface

Cloak courtyard walls with leafy plants in tubs or large pots, as well as climbers (for suitable climbing Roses, see above).

PATIO DESIGNS

The shape and size of a patio in a small garden is usually dictated by the house and garden. Don't just consider a square or rectangular shape; examples of patio shapes are illustrated below. There are designs for formal and informal gardens, including square, round, hexagonal and composite arrangements.

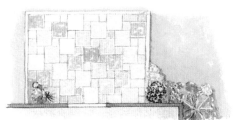
Rectangular or square patios are relatively easily constructed from regular-shaped paving – ensure there is strong edging

A composite design with a formal character, integrating a circular patio with a squared path entrance

Small circular patio made with setts

Small crazy-paved hexagon patio

Patio Roses

Roses never fail to attract attention and Patio Roses are ideal for planting along their edges. Patio Roses are a distinct group – larger and more robust than Miniature Roses, but not as large as Floribundas. Varieties to consider include:

- **'Festival':** 45 cm (1½ ft) high; semi-double, crimson-scarlet.

- **'Marlena':** 38 cm (15 in) high; long flowering period – scarlet-crimson.

- **'Sweet Dream':** 45 cm (1½ ft) high; bushy and upright, apricot-peach.

COURTYARD TUB PLANT

For a distinctive, leaf-dominant plant choose *Fatsia japonica* (False Castor Oil Plant). Its evergreen, slightly tender nature makes it ideal for planting in a tub or large pot positioned in a corner of a courtyard. The large, hand-like leaves are mid- to deep green and glossy. To highlight the leaves, plant a small-leaved, variegated Ivy behind it.

Pergolas and trellises

The large-flowered clematis 'Nelly Moser' flowers from early to late summer.

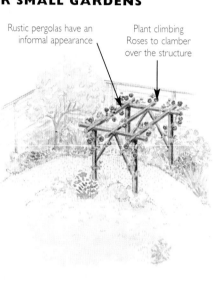

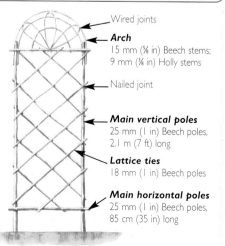

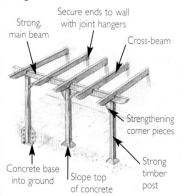

Pergola-type constructions have been known in warm countries from the earliest times, and were probably used to create shade and grow vines. The Italians adopted this concept and came up with the term pergola, meaning an arbour or walk covered mainly with vines. Trellis (derived from the French *treillage*) is latticework used to support plants and today is attached to a wall or erected as a free-standing feature to create a screen.

What are pergolas and trellises?

PERGOLAS FOR SMALL GARDENS

Pergolas can be tailored to suit small gardens, with perhaps only four upright posts and 3–4 cross-timbers straddling a path. Designs can be chosen to suit the garden's overall style, as described below.

- **Formal and traditional:** use planed timber, with square-cut ends for a clean-cut look.
- **Formal and Oriental:** use planed timber, with deeper cross-timbers chamfered at their lower ends to create an Oriental style.
- **Informal and rustic:** use rustic poles (Larch or Chestnut); thick ones for major supports and thinner ones across the top of the pergola. Also use thin poles for diagonally strengthening the corners.

Rustic pergolas have an informal appearance

Plant climbing Roses to clamber over the structure

A rustic pergola straddling a path creates an attractive focal point in a small garden.

TRELLISES IN A SMALL GARDEN

- **Wall-secured:** when securing a trellis to a wall, ensure that the framework is 36–50 mm (1½–2 in) from the surface to enable stems to pass behind it. Position the bottom of the trellis about 45 cm (18 in) above the soil and use bamboo canes to guide stems to it.
- **Free-standing trellis:** used in several ways. When cloaking a neighbouring eyesore, position a trellis 30–38 cm (12–15 in) from the fence and plant leafy climbers such as variegated, large-leaved Ivies to clamber over it. Alternatively, erect a trellis across a garden as a partition.

Small lean-to pergola

Construct a small, lean-to pergola against a wall to create a plant-covered leisure area. Secure cross-timbers to wall-brackets; a traditional, formal design is best.

Secure ends to wall with joint hangers

Strong, main beam

Cross-beam

Strengthening corner pieces

Concrete base into ground

Slope top of concrete

Strong timber post

MAKING A DECORATIVE RUSTIC TRELLIS

A small, delicate, rustic trellis with spidery woodwork was especially favoured in cottage gardens in the late nineteenth century. Here is an easily made arch; several pieces can be erected side by-side to create an eye-catching screen, perhaps separating parts of a garden. Thin Beech poles and galvanized nails are the main materials, with pliable Holly stems for the decorative top. Secure several arches together to form a long trellis.

Wired joints

Arch
15 mm (⅝ in) Beech stems; 9 mm (⅜ in) Holly stems

Nailed joint

Main vertical poles
25 mm (1 in) Beech poles, 2.1 m (7 ft) long

Lattice ties
18 mm (1 in) Beech poles

Main horizontal poles
25 mm (1 in) Beech poles, 85 cm (35 in) long

Arches and arbours

Arches, at their simplest, are just tall, inverted hoops over a path and covered in climbers, from leafy types to Roses, *Lonicera* (Honeysuckle) and Clematis. They can be constructed of planed or rustic wood, or ornamental wrought iron. Arbours have a secluded, cloistered and romantic feel, often partly covered with flowering and leafy climbers. They are usually positioned towards a corner or side and do not have to take up much room.

What are arches and arbours?

ARCHES

Arches add style to small gardens, with constructional materials ranging from rustic poles or planed wood to metal.

- Some metal arches are four-way, and are ideal for where two paths cross each other. Drench them with large-flowered Clematis.
- Latticework sides to arches with planed wood supports add a delicate touch to both formal and informal gardens. Painting the sides white or a pastel colour lends further distinction – but don't make them garish.

Rustic arch, ideal for climbing Roses

Decorative arch and semi-formal gate

Decorative wrought-iron arch

Tall-topped arch formed in a hedge

How to make a classic pergola-topped arch

Add an Oriental quality to the top of an arch by chamfering or ornately shaping the lower ends of the cross-timbers. The ends of these timbers should protrude about 23 cm (9 in) from the arch's sides.

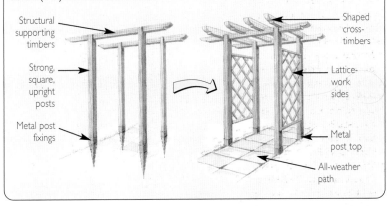

Structural supporting timbers

Strong, square, upright posts

Metal post fixings

Shaped cross-timbers

Lattice-work sides

Metal post top

All-weather path

TUNNELS

By definition, these are usually long but a 3 m (10 ft) wide tunnel only 2.4 m (8 ft) long and straddling a wide, gravel or brick path creates an attractive feature in a small garden. Clothe it with specially trained Laburnum, or apple or pear trees.

ARBOURS

There are arbours for all gardens, where they fit into corners or alongside walls or hedges. Increasingly, arbour units are sold either fully constructed or 'in the flat'. Informal ones are made of rustic poles, and formal types of sawn timber. Additionally, some are made of wrought iron and have a delicate, aged nature that suits Roses and less vigorous climbers such as *Clematis orientalis* (Oriental Clematis); *Clematis macropetala* is another choice. In a small garden, a money-saving solution for an arbour is to position a formal, wooden arch against a wall or hedge, and to fit a bench-style seat in it – for two!

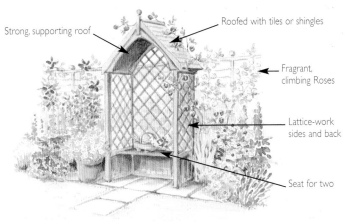

Strong, supporting roof

Roofed with tiles or shingles

Fragrant, climbing Roses

Lattice-work sides and back

Seat for two

Delightful cottage-garden type arbour, flanked by colourful informal plants in borders and against a background fence.

Porches and entrances

Will a porch complement my house?

A bare area around a front door creates the impression of neglect and blandness, but when a porch-like structure is added and clothed in flowering or leafy climbers it brightens both the house and garden. Choose a porch that harmonizes with the house, whether formal or informal. Home-made or modified shop-bought porches are easily erected, but do need to be well secured to prevent wind dislodging them when clothed with climbers.

Open-fronted porches allow light to enter the house, while protecting from rain.

Pots packed with summer-flowering plants are ideal for decorating porches.

Enclosed porches become lobbies, where many indoor plants can be grown.

DESIGN, STYLE AND MATERIALS

The design of a porch must complement the house's nature, and, while a clinically brick type may suit a modern house, a wooden one is better for older properties. Painting bricks white usually helps to impart an aged look. In narrow front gardens, a porch and fence can be treated as the same feature and constructed in similar materials.

ADDING THE FRILLS

Porch with seats

After creating the structure of a porch, it will need to be dressed in plants to soften the hard edges and add colour.
• **Flowering climbers:** choose types that harmonize with the style – those with dainty flowers for modern porches, *Lonicera* (Honeysuckle) for older properties.
• **Leafy climbers:** avoid creating a dark entrance packed with old, dusty climbers. For a summer-only display, plant the herbaceous *Humulus lupulus* 'Aureus' (Yellow-leaved Hop).
• **Hanging-baskets:** if space allows, suspend a pair of baskets where they cannot be knocked.
• **Tubs and pots:** group a few to one side of an entrance, at a variety of different heights.

HOW TO MAKE A RUSTIC PORCH

Some porches are easily made and fixed into position. Construct an informal porch from four chestnut rustic poles (each about 2.4 m (8 ft) long and two poles (for the top), each 1.5 m (5 ft) long. Add strengthening cross-poles lower down and at the sides. Pieces of expanded trellis are needed for the sides and top. The supporting poles are concreted into the ground to a depth of 45 cm (18 in).

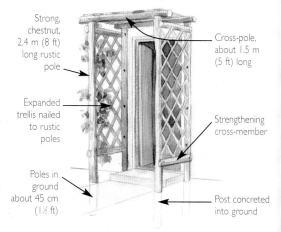

Strong, chestnut, 2.4 m (8 ft) long rustic pole

Cross-pole, about 1.5 m (5 ft) long

Expanded trellis nailed to rustic poles

Strengthening cross-member

Poles in ground about 45 cm (1½ ft)

Post concreted into ground

Edgings for borders and paths

Edgings have both functional and artistic value, and mark the edges of borders, lawns and paths. Some border edgings help to retain soil, while those combined with mowing strips are both functional and artistic. They help to protect lawn edges and make mowing easier and quicker, without damage to cutting blades. The options of materials are wide, from wooden logs and bricks to ornate edgings ideal for flower borders. Secure installation is essential.

Are edgings necessary?

BORDER EDGING OPTIONS

- Traditionally, edges of lawns when next to a border were initially cut with an edging iron (edging knife) and throughout summer long grass was trimmed with edging shears. This works well, but edges often become damaged.
- Edges of lawns abutting herbaceous borders sometimes become bare and unsightly when leaves of plants trespass on them. One solution is to install a row of 30 cm (12 in) wide paving slabs along them. It also makes lawns easier to cut.

Concrete, cast and coloured to resemble cappings on walls, is readily available

Rope-top tiles are Victorian in style; ensure they are well secured

Round-top concrete slabs have a formal nature; ideal for straight edgings

Low, picket-type edgings need an informal garden with dainty flower beds

Weather-resistant bricks set at a 45° angle make an attractive border edging.

NEXT TO WALLS

A lawn immediately next to a wall or fence makes it difficult to manoeuvre a mowing machine and to cut grass. The same problem arises next to a retaining wall. The solution is to install a 30 cm (12 in) wide mowing strip of bricks or paving slabs. Ensure that their surfaces are level with the lawn.

Edgings with mowing strips

Mowing strips that separate border soil from a lawn enable grass to be easily cut; their surfaces need to be level with the lawn to prevent damage to the mower's blades.

UNUSUAL EDGINGS

Paths with log edgings have an informal nature

In rustic areas, grass paths are attractive when edged with logs partly buried in the soil. However, as grass at the edges of log paths is time-consuming to trim, an alternative is shingle or shredded bark. The disadvantage is that birds sometimes scatter the bark. Large pebbles cemented into position alongside a patio or firm-surfaced path are attractive and ideal for semi-informal areas.

Pebble edgings are informal and novel

CURVED EDGING

↗ *Strips of metal-linked rustic logs are ideal for informal curved edgings*

↗ *Brick edging with pebble in-filling is inexpensive and good for curved paths*

RETAINING SOIL

When the level of soil in a border is above that of a lawn or path, use rolls of strong logs. Install them to about one-third of their depth in a trench, return the soil and thoroughly firm it. Low brick walls are another solution, but need strong foundations and take longer to create. Nevertheless, they are stronger and longer-lived than rolls of logs; they are best reserved for straight-edge borders.

Bricks and pavers are attractive, but difficult to lay in a curve.

Sheds and summerhouses

In a large garden, a shed is essential for storing tools, pots and composts. In a small garden, a combined shed and summerhouse is a solution, or a shed with a glazed side that enables seedlings and plants to be raised in spring. Where there is a garage, this often acts as a store for gardening tools (do not store fruit or vegetables in a garage as they may absorb fumes from stored fuel or a car). Whatever is used, it must be dry and vermin-proof, with a good circulation of air.

SHEDS

There are sheds in all sizes and shapes; for a small garden, you should choose a compact but practical one. Some are just box-like and only slightly wider than the door. Because they are small but nevertheless have a tall structure, a secure base is essential and preferably a wind-sheltered position.

A small, apex-roofed shed

A modestly sized, pent-roofed shed

STORAGE BOXES

For tiny gardens with perhaps only a patio and small plot of land, a large storage box is ideal. These have a waterproof, sloped, hinged top and are up to 1.8 m (6 ft) long.

SUMMERHOUSES

These are popular, but only small ones are possible – try a shape that fits into a corner. In a small garden, they create storage places for garden tools, as well as leisure areas for solitude and viewing the garden. A summerhouse therefore must be attractive and, perhaps, create a focal point. A paved surround is ideal for chairs and tables.

Summerhouses bring an upmarket quality, as well as being leisure and storage areas.

Gazebo or summerhouse?

Both gazebos and summerhouses have distinctive qualities, but whereas a gazebo has open sides – or sometimes partly enclosed by attractive latticework – a summerhouse has windows and doors.

Both of these structures need careful positioning and whereas a gazebo can be positioned well into a garden, a summerhouse is best when close to a boundary. Bandstands – a legacy from earlier days when musicians regularly played in parks – have a similar nature to gazebos but with open views on all sides.

Cladding

Wide range, from 'feather-edged' through 'tongued-and-grooved' to 'barrelled', which gives the impression of a log cabin. Before buying a wooden garden building, inspect sheds at a timber merchant or builder's yard and compare prices.

SPACE-SAVING COMBINATIONS

- A combined shed and summerhouse is one space-saving solution, perhaps with a small verandah and paved leisure area.
- A shed with a glazed side that enables summer-flowering bedding plants to be raised in spring (gentle warmth and good ventilation are essential). However, line bench surfaces with plastic sheeting to prevent excess water dripping on the floor. Alternatively, use large, shallow, plastic trays.

Summerhouses are often play areas for children

A practical solution to lack of space (see left)

PLAYHOUSES

Children love their own playhouse. Permanent ones are usually constructed of wood, with acrylic or PVC windows. Safety is essential and all sharp corners, screws and nails must be made safe. Small, temporary playhouses built of rigid plastic are available.

MAINTENANCE

To reduce maintenance on a shed or summerhouse made of 'deal' (a softwood), make sure the timber has been pressure-treated with a wood preservative. This impregnates the timber and makes it more resistant to decay, which is inevitable with this type of wood.

Greenhouses and cloches

Greenhouses add a further dimension to your gardening and will enable a wider range of plants to be grown. Even the smallest structure can be used to raise summer-flowering bedding plants in late winter and spring. If the space required for a greenhouse is simply not available, a few cloches will facilitate earlier sowing of vegetable seeds in spring, as well as extending the ripening and maturing of plants in late summer and early autumn.

Do I need a greenhouse?

GREENHOUSES

Lean-to and mini greenhouses are popular in small gardens and are best given a sun-facing position with shelter from strong, cold winds. Hexagonal greenhouses have a novel outline and need an open position; use them as centrepieces in a vegetable garden. Ensure that the door is facing away from the prevailing wind. If space allows, even-span greenhouses are popular, as most of their area can be used to grow plants. Strong staging – made from wood or angled metal – is essential to enable plants to be looked after. Staging 60 cm (2 ft) wide is best.

Lean-to greenhouses are popular, but there must be good ventilation in the roof and sides.

Mini-greenhouses need regular attention, as the temperature rapidly fluctuates.

SHADING GREENHOUSES

All greenhouses need to be shaded in summer, especially small ones in which the temperature fluctuates throughout the day. Either drape plastic-coated sheeting over the outside or coat the glass with white shading. Remove all shading in autumn.

MATERIALS

Modern greenhouses are usually made of extruded aluminium, which allows the maximum amount of light to enter. It is also maintenance-free. Panes of glass are held in position by metal clips, which spring into position. Wood is also popular – Western Red Cedar is durable; instead of being painted it is annually cleaned and coated in linseed oil. Wooden greenhouses are ideal for informal, cottage-type gardens, where they harmonize with their surroundings better than metal types.

GREENHOUSE KNOWHOW

- Keep the glass clean throughout the year, especially in early spring.
- Clean gutters in autumn to prevent leaves and dirty water being trapped.
- In autumn or early winter, remove all plant debris and thoroughly wash the inside. Then, leave the door and ventilators open for a few weeks.
- During winter, check that ventilators open and close properly; if automatic ventilators are fitted, check that they are working. Also ensure that the door opens and closes easily.
- If an electrical supply has been installed in the greenhouse, have it checked by a competent electrician, ready for seed sowing in late winter and spring.

CLOCHES

Compared with a greenhouse, cloches in a small garden are far more versatile, as well as cheaper. In late winter, they can be placed over prepared soil to encourage it to warm up quickly so that early crops can be sown. In autumn, they extend the growing and maturing season. Years ago, cloches were chiefly made of glass, but more recently polythene sheeting and corrugated PVC have been introduced.

Bell-jars

➜ *These were traditionally made of glass, but modern adaptations of the bell-jar are formed out of transparent plastic. Large, clear plastic bottles with their bases cut off are often used as well.*

Barn cloches

↗ *Barn cloches are formed of four sheets of glass, held in place by metal clips.*

Corrugated PVC cloches

↗ *These are light and strong, although they are vulnerable to gusty wind.*

Glossary

Annual A plant that grows from seed, flowers and dies within the same year. However, many plants that are not strictly annuals are treated as such. For instance, *Lobelia erinus* is a half-hardy perennial usually grown as a half-hardy annual.

Balled plants A way in which plants are sometimes sold. Mainly conifers or small evergreen shrubs with hessian tightly wrapped around the rootball. They are usually sold during late summer and early autumn, or in spring.

Bamboos Collective name for a group of plants in the grass family. They have stiff canes (some spectacularly coloured or shaped) and attractive leaves (often brightly coloured).

Bare-rooted plants A way in which plants are sometimes sold. Deciduous shrubs or trees dug up from a nursery bed in winter, when they are bare of leaves. They are replanted in their growing positions as soon as possible.

Bedding plant A plant raised and used as a seasonal feature in a border or bed. Spring-flowering plants are planted in autumn for spring display and include biennials such as Wallflowers and bulbs like Tulips. Summer-flowering bedding plants are usually half-hardy annuals raised under glass in gentle warmth in late winter or early spring. Plants are acclimatized to outdoor conditions and planted into borders and containers when all risk of frost has passed.

Biennial A plant with a two-year growing cycle, raised from seeds sown during one year for flowering in the following one.

Bud A tightly packed and closed immature shoot or flower.

Bulb A storage organ with a bud-like structure. It is formed of fleshy scales attached at their bases to a basal plate. Onions and Tulips are examples of bulbs.

Bulbil An immature and miniature bulb at the base of a mother bulb.

Container gardening Growing plants in containers, from pots and tubs to wall-baskets, hanging-baskets and windowboxes. Some of these are permanent features, others seasonal.

Container-grown plants A way in which plants are sometimes sold. Plants established and growing in a container – may be evergreen or deciduous shrubs or trees, or herbaceous perennials or rock-garden plants. They can be planted at any time of the year when the soil and weather are suitable.

Corm A storage organ formed of a stem base greatly swollen laterally. A good example is a Gladiolus. Young corms (cormlets) form around its base, and can be removed and grown in a nursery bed for several seasons until large enough to be planted into a flowering position.

Cultivar A variety raised in cultivation, rather than appearing naturally without any interference from man.

Deadheading The removal of faded flowerheads to prevent the formation of seeds and to encourage a plant to direct all of its energies into growth and flowering.

Deciduous Shrubs and trees (and some conifers and climbers) that shed their leaves in autumn and produce a fresh array in spring. A few slightly tender evergreens lose some of their leaves during very severe weather.

Earthing up The drawing up of soil around the base of a plant to exclude light or to support it against buffeting wind. Chiefly used for potatoes and celery.

Evergreen Plants that retain their leaves throughout the year and therefore always appear green. However, they regularly lose leaves, while producing further ones.

F1 The first filial generation: the result of a cross between two pure-bred parents. F1 hybrids are large and strong plants, but their seeds will not produce replicas of the parents.

Fertilization The sexual union of the male cell (pollen) and the female cell (ovule). Fertilization may be the result of pollination (when pollen falls on the stigma, a female part of a flower).

Form A loose and rather non-botanical term used to refer to a variation with a particular species.

Hardening off The gradual acclimatizing of tender plants to outside conditions. Garden frames are useful for this purpose.

Hardy Able to survive winter outdoors in a temperate climate.

Heeling-in Covering the roots of bare-rooted shrubs and trees with soil while waiting to be planted.

Herbaceous A plant that dies down to soil level in autumn or early winter, after the completion of each season's growth. Fresh shoots develop in spring.

Hybrid A plant resulting from a cross between two distinct varieties, subspecies or genera.

Layering A vegetative method of increasing plants by lowering stems and burying them in the ground. By twisting, bending or slitting the stem at the point where it is buried, the flow of sap is restricted and roots induced to form.

Mulching Covering soil around plants with a thick layer of well-decayed organic material such as garden compost and manure.

Pruning The controlled removal of stems or shoots to encourage a plant to form a better shape, develop fruits and flowers and, in a few instances, develop attractive stems.

Shrub A woody plant with several stems coming from ground level.

Standard A plant grown on a single stem, with a long, bare area between the ground and the lowest branch. Many fruit trees and roses are grown as standard trees.

Stooling Cutting down woody stems to just above soil level to encourage the development of young, fresh shoots. Some shrubs and trees are regularly treated in this way, including Willows and Dogwoods.

Subsoil Soil below the normal depth at which the area is cultivated.

Topsoil The top layer of soil in which most plants grow.

Tree A woody-stemmed plant with a clear stem (trunk) between the roots and the lowest branch.

Trunk The main stem of a tree.

Tuber An underground storage organ, such as that of a Dahlia.

Variegated Mainly applied to leaves and used to describe a state of having two or more colours.

Variety A naturally occurring variation within a plant species.

Weeping Having a cascading habit, and used to describe the outline of a tree or conifer. Some roses are grown as weeping standards.

Index

Acknowledgments

AG&G Books would like to thank the following for their contribution: **Bradshaws**, **OASE** and **Thompson & Morgan**, Quality Seedsmen Since 1855, *brings the finest quality flower and vegetable seed and flower plant varieties to the home gardener*, Thompson & Morgan (UK) Ltd, Poplar Lane, Ipswich, Suffolk, IP8 3BU. Photographs: AG&G Books (pages 3BC, 6, 10TR, 13, 16, 18, 20TL, 22, 26, 27, 32, 36BL, 47BL AND BR, 49BR, 51C, 61, 64, 70, 71, 74 and 75), Bradshaws (page 14 EXCEPT C), Garden Matters (pages 56BC, 57TL AND TR), Peter McHoy (front of cover and pages 35TC, 42BR, 50BL, 50BC, 52BR, 53BL, 56BR, 57BL, 58BC, 59TC, 59TR), OASE (page 14C), David Squire (all pictures except those listed here) and Thompson & Morgan (page 35TR, 36BC, 58BR and 59BL).